# Life Skills For Teenage Girls

Advice on Being More Confident, Dating, Managing Your Money, Dealing With Peer Pressure, Healthy Relationships, and Other Skills

## Pathways Press

© Copyright 2023 - All rights reserved.

The content contained within this book may not be reproduced, duplicated or transmitted without direct written permission from the author or the publisher.

Under no circumstances will any blame or legal responsibility be held against the publisher, or author, for any damages, reparation, or monetary loss due to the information contained within this book, either directly or indirectly.

Legal Notice:
This book is copyright protected. It is only for personal use. You cannot amend, distribute, sell, use, quote or paraphrase any part, or the content within this book, without the consent of the author or publisher.

Disclaimer Notice:
Please note the information contained within this document is for educational and entertainment purposes only. All effort has been executed to present accurate, up to date, reliable, complete information. No warranties of any kind are declared or implied. Readers acknowledge that the author is not engaged in the rendering of legal, financial, medical or professional advice. The content within this book has been derived from various sources. Please consult a licensed professional before attempting any techniques outlined in this book.

By reading this document, the reader agrees that under no circumstances is the author responsible for any losses, direct or indirect, that are incurred as a result of the use of the information contained within this document, including, but not limited to, errors, omissions, or inaccuracies.

# Table of Contents

| | |
|---|---|
| Introduction | 1 |
| Chapter 1: How To Start | 4 |
|   Knowing Your Worth | 4 |
|   How to Talk to Yourself | 8 |
|   Dealing With Peer Pressure | 11 |
|     So What Is Peer Pressure? | 11 |
|     What Are The Defenses Against Harmful Peer Pressure? | 12 |
|   Surrounding Yourself With the Right People | 14 |
|     How to Make Friends | 14 |
|     Making Friends if You're Shy | 16 |
|     Toxic Relationships | 16 |
|     Options to Deal With a Toxic Friendship | 19 |
| Chapter 2: Personal Care and Listening to Your Changing Body | 22 |
|   Skincare | 22 |
|     Sunscreen | 23 |
|     Shaving | 24 |
|   Basic Grooming | 27 |
|     Hair Care Tips | 27 |
|     Trimming Your Nails | 29 |
|   Makeup | 30 |
|     Disadvantages of Makeup | 30 |
|     Basic Makeup Items | 31 |
|     Makeup Tips for Beginners | 32 |
|   Tackling Unpleasant Odors | 32 |
|     Bad Breath | 33 |
|     Body Odor | 33 |
|   How To Shop for a Bra | 34 |
|     Finding the Correct Bra | 34 |
|     Getting the Right Measurements | 35 |
|     Perfect Fitting Bra | 36 |
|   All About Your Period | 37 |
|     What's Your Period? | 37 |
|     How to Manage Your Period | 38 |
|     How Do I Choose What to Employ? | 40 |
|     Products to Relieve Menstrual Pain | 40 |
|     Quick Period Hacks | 40 |
|     Outfit Ideas to Stay Comfortable During Your Period | 42 |
|     Problems to Watch Out For | 42 |

## Chapter 3: The Power of Politeness — 45
### The Importance of Good Manners — 45
### Social Etiquette — 48
- How to Shake Hands — 48
- Strategies for Improving Your Business Handshake — 49
- How to Introduce Yourself — 50
- How to Introduce Yourself in a Job Interview — 51
- How to Introduce Yourself to a Recruiter in an Email — 51
- Tips for Introducing Others — 52
- Restaurant Etiquette and Table Manners — 53
- How to Leave a Tip — 54

## Chapter 4: The Delicate Discussing of Dating and Daughters — 58
### How to Confess Your Feelings Without Making Things Weird — 58
### Cute Ways to Ask Your Crush Out — 60
### Planning Your First Date — 61
- Before You Start Dating — 62
- The Initial Date — 62
- Lust vs. Love — 62
- Tips for Teen Dating — 62
### Fun, Non-Awkward First Date Ideas — 63
### Dating Advice — 65
- Know (and Be) Who You Are — 66
- Never Ask For Love — 66
- Avoid Rushing — 66
- Create Boundaries — 66
- Never Let Your Standards Slip — 67
- Remember Your Friends — 67
- Don't Run Away From Issues — 67
- Learn How to Spot Toxic Relationships — 67
- Improve One Another's Quality of Life — 68
- Love Isn't Sex — 68
### Safety Tips — 68
- Have a Curfew — 68
- Negotiate Ground Rules — 69
- Let Your Parents Meet Your Date — 69
- Let Your Parents Be a Standing Excuse for You — 69
- Let Others Know Where You Are — 69
### How To Respectfully Break Up With Someone — 69
- Break-Up Dos and Don'ts — 70
- How to Speak and What to Say — 71

## Chapter 5: How to Land Your First Job Like a Pro — 74
### Choosing the Perfect Job for You — 74

| | |
|---|---|
| Types of Jobs for Teenagers | 74 |
| Determine What Type of Job You Want | 75 |
| Where to Look for Jobs | 75 |
| Start Building Your Network | 76 |
| How to Apply for a Job | 76 |
| Get a Work Permit | 76 |
| Make a Resume | 76 |
| Add a Cover Letter | 78 |
| Submit Applications | 80 |
| Prepare for Interviews or Job Tests | 81 |
| General Tips for Applying for Jobs as a Teenager | 84 |
| Chapter 6: Managing Your Money Matters | 88 |
| Budgeting 101 | 88 |
| How to Create a Budget | 89 |
| Budgeting Tips | 90 |
| How to Build a Savings Account | 91 |
| Joint Accounts | 91 |
| Teen Savings Account | 91 |
| Uniform Transfer to Minor Act | 91 |
| Options for Withdrawing Money from Your Savings | 92 |
| Advice to Start Creating Better Money Habits | 92 |
| Use Time Well | 92 |
| Get Into the Saving Habit | 93 |
| Avoid Unnecessary Spending | 93 |
| Healthy Money Relationships | 94 |
| Consider College | 94 |
| Take Advantage of Your Student ID | 94 |
| Taxation | 95 |
| Preventing Debt | 95 |
| Teen Financial Planning | 95 |
| Avoid Identity Theft | 96 |
| Chapter 7: Surviving Being Home Alone | 98 |
| How to Do Laundry | 98 |
| Steps to Doing Laundry Properly | 98 |
| Common Laundry Problems and How to Fix Them | 100 |
| How to Iron Stuff | 102 |
| Ironing a T-Shirt | 102 |
| Ironing Pants | 103 |
| Ironing Skirts and Dresses | 103 |
| Ironing Tips | 104 |
| How to Sew a Button | 104 |
| Hand Sewing: Thread and Tie | 105 |

| | |
|---|---|
| How to Clean a Bathroom | 106 |
|     Cleaning Supplies | 106 |
|     Cleaning the Bathroom | 106 |
| Finding Your Way Around the Kitchen | 107 |
|     Safety | 107 |
|     Expiry Dates | 109 |
|     Kitchen Safety | 110 |
| **Chapter 8: The Responsibilities of Owning and Driving a Car** | **115** |
| Importance of Driving Responsibly | 115 |
|     Teen Drivers Statistics | 115 |
|     Risk Factors | 116 |
|     Driving Safety Tips | 117 |
| Things You Should Know How to Do Before Getting Behind the Wheel | 117 |
|     Check Tire Pressure and Tread Wear | 118 |
|     How to Change a Tire | 118 |
|     How to Replace Windshield Wipers | 119 |
|     Check Fluids | 119 |
|     Jump-Starting a Car | 120 |
|     How to Respond to an Emergency | 121 |
|     How to Handle the "Check Engine" Light | 121 |
|     Car Dashboard Symbols | 121 |
|     What to Do After an Accident | 122 |
|     Driving in Rain and Snow | 122 |
|     The Importance of Preventive Maintenance | 122 |
| What to Do When You Get Pulled Over by a Cop | 122 |
|     Pullover Procedure | 122 |
| **Conclusion** | **126** |
| **Glossary** | **127** |
| **References** | **128** |

# Introduction

### It takes courage to grow up and become who you really are.
### –E. E. Cummings

— ♥ — ▲ — ♥ — ▲ — ♥ —

Growing up can be scary, and if we're being honest, it occasionally sucks. It can be a mortifying time of your life when you have boobs out of nowhere, your face starts breaking out, and let's not forget that pesky little visitor you get every month. But the reality still remains that we can't stay a kid forever. In fact, a famous quote from Gail Carson Levine says, "When you become a teenager, you step onto a bridge. You may already be on it. The opposite shore is adulthood. Childhood lies behind. The bridge is made of wood. As you cross, it burns behind you" (Goodreads, n.d.).

While Gail Carson Levine's metaphor could not be more accurate, it also couldn't be more... horrifying! It can be truly frightening to think that nothing will ever be the same again. But we must all cross that bridge.

There are both good and bad things about growing up. Growing out of the title "kid" and being seen as a young adult can be quite satisfying. But it can also be stressful and horrendous when the pressures of life and adulthood come crashing down, especially when you don't see it coming. It's true that growing up seems like a scam sometimes, but if you are equipped the right way and prepared for what's to come, you'll be just fine in the end.

And this book is here to show you how to do that.

With tips on how to deal with anything from practical skills to dealing with personal issues, this book will help you stand on your own two feet and make the most of your teenage years.

It'll help you learn more about yourself and provide the answers to those crucial questions that you might be reluctant to ask your parents. It will also teach you about the essential life skills you'll need as you develop more independence and responsibility as a teenager. The core skills and knowledge that you'll gain will enable them to succeed and eventually live independently. It'll empower you to live your life with confidence and purpose, knowing that you have learned essential skills needed to cross that bridge of childhood to adulthood without feeling compelled to look back.

And don't worry. This doesn't mean you have to ditch watching cartoons, throw out your *Toy Story* action figures (since they still haven't warmed up to you enough to cut the act and come to life yet), or start wearing business suits and walking around with briefcases. No. Growing up and acquiring life skills doesn't mean losing your innocence or becoming "boring." You're still young with your whole life ahead of you, and you ought to embrace and enjoy your youth. But it won't hurt to do so while learning the skills, tricks, and tactics shared in this book.

Having been teenagers once upon a time, we realize how important it is to be as involved in a child's life as possible, even if they are not your own. We've learned so much about not only watching a teen grow up but helping them in the most loving and essential way possible. It's our aim to help teenagers worldwide access their full potential, steer them in the right direction to adulthood, and let them know that we are here for them as a friend, mentor, and listening ear. So, not only have we equipped this book with extensive research and effective strategies, information, and tactics to bring across a clear message and substantial book, but it is also clothed with love, determination, and passion for helping you in this important transition from childhood to adulthood.

The first four chapters will focus on more personal, intrinsic issues like self-care, relationships, and taking care of your emotional, physical, and mental health. The final four chapters will get more practical, giving you substance about real-life skills that you'll need to tackle the world and make it out on top in the end.

The end goal is to ensure that you are right on your way to a bright future, knowing more than you did a few weeks ago and confident enough to tackle the world.

Maybe you haven't the faintest idea of what you want to do when you're older, or maybe you're at the brink of college and still have no clue what career path to choose. And that's okay. It'll get better… not easier, but better. So make some friends, get a new hobby, start something that you're bad at until you're pretty good at it, and most of all, invest in your future, no matter how small. And hey, don't worry if you haven't as yet. This book can be your very first investment in the you of tomorrow as you grow yourself with the eight chapters of this book.

No one can choose for you, so decide today to start being the person you want to be. Your future self will thank you for it.

# Chapter 1: How To Start

> YOU ARE VERY POWERFUL,
> PROVIDED YOU KNOW HOW POWERFUL YOU ARE.
> —YOGI BHAJAN

We might easily overlook the above quote, saying, "Oh, it's just another cliche bundle of words that an old guy said a hundred years ago." And maybe, to an extent, you're right. But when we examine the words deeply and apply them to ourselves, we see the true meaning behind them. Hearing that you are powerful and believing such are two completely different things, and when we believe these words, you would be surprised at how far they can take you. This is the first step in paving your way to a bigger, brighter future as a young adult.

The teenage years are crucial as you learn who you really are and who your true friends are. Your identity, likes, dislikes, and maybe even your life partner change after just five years. If you let it, this can be the best time of your life. Like The Three Little Pigs, constructing a strong foundation is the best way to weather a storm. This, in all its entirety, are the choices you make in your teenage years. So, if you read between the lines of the quote, you realize that it really is saying that if you don't believe in yourself, no amount of praise can make you feel like you're good enough. Haters can't defeat you if you believe in yourself. Because when you believe it, you'll feel powerful, strong, and beautiful. This is the most crucial life skill, and you should always endeavor to improve it.

So, in this chapter, we will start off by helping you build the most important skill and foundation of your life, and that's by building your perception of your worth.

### Knowing Your Worth

These days, too many teens forfeit their ability to succeed and advance in life due to a basic lack of self-confidence. They question themselves, feel unworthy, and never pursue their aspirations. Thus, they live mediocre lives.

But this doesn't need to be the case. Not if you use these confidence-boosting life hacks immediately.

Confidence is essential. If you believe passionately enough, you can do anything.

During puberty, your body changes, and you probably feel less confident than you'd like. You may have thought you'd never fit into your prom dress, wear white pants, or have the haircut you've always wanted. But although the past cannot be changed, there is still time, and the clock is still running.

Take advantage of this list of confidence boosters. They can assist you in gaining the self-assurance you'll need to change the course of your life.

## PUT SELF-COMPASSION FIRST (NOT SELF-ESTEEM)

Believing in self-esteem is risky since it measures your worth on a broad scale. You may wonder, "Am I up to par? How do I stack up against my peers?"

But treating yourself with kindness, openness, and acceptance is a healthy substitute for the constant striving and performance-oriented mindset frequently associated with self-esteem. Instead of criticism, try compassion by saying, "It's okay; I tried my best."

## BUILD ON SPECIAL SKILLS

Track your skills and interests. If you're good at gymnastics or making hair accessories, focus on them and commit to improving. This doesn't mean you should quit a skill you're not good at; however, developing a talent can increase your self-esteem.

## REPROGRAM YOURSELF

If you're still discovering yourself, reprogramming yourself may seem strange. But the truth is, the true definition of confidence is a firm belief in oneself. When you convince yourself that you can do or deserve something, your chances of success increase considerably. Thus, you must convince yourself that you deserve the life you want at whatever age.

## HELP OTHERS, ESPECIALLY STRANGERS

Helping others makes you confident and strong. However, this shouldn't be done selfishly. Do it because you want to help and not because you want to feel better about yourself. You'll feel more energized, self-assured, and involved in your neighborhood or school.

## CREATE A GOAL AND PURSUE IT

What was your goal at the start of the school year? Did you accomplish it? It's okay if you didn't. Simply set a more manageable goal. Most goals will force you to grow, even if you don't reach them. Persistence and dedication will help you succeed in all areas of life and build confidence.

## SPEND SOME TIME ON YOURSELF

By isolating yourself, you can filter out the daily noise that hinders you from being who you want to be. Thus, spending time alone and listening to your thoughts might boost self-awareness.

## HAVE A COLD SHOWER

This odd trick can actually boost confidence. Awakening your sympathetic nerve system in a cold shower reduces depression. Thus, a cold shower will flood your brain with signals and endorphins, making you happier. Happiness boosts confidence.

## CALM YOUR MIND

Meditation clears your mind since it requires focus and stillness. If done correctly, it may soothe your anxious thoughts. So, take a moment to think. Meditation and walking will improve your day and mood.

## STEP AWAY FROM YOUR COMFORT ZONE

We challenge ourselves when we try new things. We gain new perspectives by leaving our comfort zones. Changes in thought can boost confidence, too. When we leave our comfort zones, we might have fascinating new experiences that enhance our confidence and vitality.

## GET IN SHAPE

Physical activity improves mental wellness. You'll create a good cycle of discipline and confidence by improving your appearance. Physical improvement will lead to mental improvement.

## ACCEPT SPONTANEITY

Most people have daily routines. However, to increase your confidence, you should be prepared for things to be a little challenging at first. You should feel comfortable changing things up a bit.

## PRACTICE, PRACTICE, PRACTICE

We often doubt ourselves because we don't think we're capable. However, if you practice, you can overcome nervous thoughts. Thus, if you study a subject thoroughly, you will be better prepared to practice it.

## ALWAYS GIVE YOUR BEST

When you work hard, confidence comes easily. Giving something your all and doing your best eliminates insecurity. Full effort equals achievement. This attitude will build confidence.

## WALK FASTER

This confidence hack is strange but effective. Walking with purpose, which speeds you up, usually boosts self-esteem. Try this confidence tactic even if you are skeptical.

## ENGAGE IN GROUP ACTIVITIES

Teamwork boosts self-confidence easily. Working as a team in a sport (yes, ladies can play sports!), debate team, or glee club can aid you in college and your future goals. You'll also learn to speak up and build community, which boosts self-esteem.

## RECEIVE AND GIVE COMPLIMENTS

You must be comfortable accepting compliments. It's alright to be shy at first, but the next time a classmate appreciates your outfit, accept it and reciprocate the compliment.

## LEARN MORE ABOUT CONFIDENCE

Far too many individuals mistakenly think that confidence is a trait you are born with. This isn't the case, though. Unintentional and intended learning events build confidence.

Learn about confidence by reading uplifting content, watching videos, or studying yourself.

# How to Talk to Yourself

Speaking to yourself, whether out loud or internally, is known as self-talk. These are the words you are constantly feeding your mind about yourself, whether they be positive or negative.

The thoughts you have about yourself can either inspire and motivate you if they are positive or limit you if they are pessimistic.

Self-talk is crucial, as it conveys the messages that decide whether you should persist in your efforts or not. Therefore, it is crucial that we let the words we speak to ourselves be nothing less than positive.

Here are thirteen suggestions to help your self-tak become successful and positive.

## STAY POSITIVE

"Oh my! Why didn't I think of that!" you might've said when you read this heading. Seems obvious, right? However, we often talk to ourselves when thinking. Thus, positive self-talk is essential.

It's hard to always think positively about yourself. But you can replace negative thoughts with positive ones. Every circumstance has an upside or an opposite. Start finding the good to turn your negatives into positives.

## HAVE A PURPOSE GREATER THAN YOURSELF

Believing in a higher force generates positive thinking.

If you believe God (or a higher force) loves you, you will think better of yourself. A strong being created you for a purpose. This, of course, can extend beyond religion. It can be a great connection with yourself and your own mind. When you truly believe this, you are more likely to have self-confidence and pursue your life goals.

## BE GRATEFUL

Gratitude helps you see the good in your life and generate positive self-talk. Practicing gratitude daily will improve your self-talk. You'll be happier too.

Keep a gratitude notebook to cultivate thankfulness. Record your gratitude daily.

## NEVER COMPARE YOURSELF TO OTHERS

Let's admit it. We've all compared ourselves to someone before, whether it was a celebrity, an older sibling or cousin, or even our peers. It's okay if it happens once or twice, but don't let it get you down. Comparing yourself to someone and seeing everything "great" about them and awful about yourself is detrimental. Comparing yourself to others might lead to depression. Instead of complaining, be grateful for what you have.

Everyone has it, better or worse. It's more important to appreciate yourself and your life.

## USE POSITIVE WORDS WITH OTHERS

If we're rude to others, we're more likely to think poorly of ourselves. Start speaking positively and share affirmations with everyone you care about, starting with yourself. This will transform your attitude.

## POSITIVITY FOR YOUR SUCCESS

Have faith in your abilities and your capacity for success so you may propel yourself toward achievement. Doubting yourself prevents you from trying, which prevents you from succeeding. Even if it takes several attempts, have faith that you can succeed.

Who will believe in you if not yourself?

## DON'T BE AFRAID OF FAILURE

Yes, I know it's scary to get back that test paper and dread the big red F that Timmy always gets in The Fairly OddParents. However, failure often leads to success. Several great success stories feature people who failed many times before succeeding. If they gave up after failing once, they would never have succeeded. Failure may be terrifying, painful, and costly, but there's always a lesson. Fearing leads to crippling and doubting, which can affect how you talk to yourself.

You'll succeed if you utilize failure to try again and change tactics.

## POST UPLIFTING AFFIRMATIONS

Have inspirational sayings, verses, and affirmations written down, and post them somewhere you can see them frequently during the day, such as on your refrigerator, bathroom mirror, or right next to your computer.

Here are some affirmations you can use to get started:

- Every day, I nourish my spirit.
- How I feel right now is up to me.
- I'm appreciative of...
- Today, I'll go with thankfulness and joy.
- I am kind to myself and to other people.
- I matter and serve a function in this universe.

## USE A VOICE OF INSTRUCTION

As students, you can use instructional self-talk to stay on task or to regain attention after making a mistake. However, remember to speak gently and patiently. Don't be a yelling teacher or a self-critic. Having an instructional voice doesn't mean bullying yourself.

Instructional self-talk emphasizes techniques to improve a skill. "Keep your head up and don't react to the bully" is all you need to start.

## MOVE AWAY FROM THE PAST

Take it easy on yourself. Everyone has a past and has had bad experiences. So, don't dwell on your mistakes.

Imagine yourself in a spaceship, going to explore the galaxy. But in order to see the wonders of the universe, you have to leave your luggage at the entrance. This is like life. At this age, you can travel the world, but your history can hold you back. However, you may leave it and your negative ideas and self-talk at the door.

Focus on the future, especially good things.

## IMAGINE YOUR SUCCESS

We all have an imagination. Most times, it conjures up things that can never happen, like flying pigs, cats who accept that they are the pets and not in charge, or flies and mosquitoes not being obnoxious. However, your creativity isn't restricted to fairytales and unattainable things. Visualizing success helps you achieve it.

When you imagine, it motivates you to think positively about your circumstances and to believe that your goals are achievable.

### DREAM AND SET OBJECTIVES

Dreaming about the future is a fantastic technique to start using positive self-talk. What do you want out of life? What do you hope to achieve in life? Where do you see yourself in five, ten, or fifteen years?

Dream big, then create attainable goals to get there. Completing these little tasks will boost your confidence and foster positive self-talk. Try not to beat yourself up if you fail. Allow flexibility and plan changes for happiness. Remind yourself that it's okay to give up aspirations and pursue others. Life is yours.

## Dealing With Peer Pressure

Everybody has friends. They are roughly your age and have similar interests and experiences that pull you guys together. Peers can also be kids your age who participate in the same activities as you do or who are a part of the same community or group. Even if you don't regard all of your peers as friends, they might still have an impact on you.

### SO WHAT IS PEER PRESSURE?

Peer pressure is when someone tries to persuade you to act a certain way or do something. Even if they are not pressuring you, you can still desire to act like your peers, like the desire to blend in.

Sometimes, peer pressure can be good, like studying, because almost all the class is studying, but most times, it's negative. The best thing to do is to be who you are, even if that means standing out from your peers.

Below are some examples of harmful peer pressure:

- changing your values to please the crowd
- being dishonest in your school work and tests
- theft or shoplifting
- bullying or associating with others who treat your peers badly
- risky driving

- catfishing on social media or being inappropriate
- using drugs and other substances
- getting involved in sexual acts because everyone else is doing it

So how do you know if it's peer pressure or not? Let's identify some characteristics:

- If you were forced to do something that you simply didn't want to do.
- If people you usually hang out with don't recognize you.
- If your peers have hurt your feelings or made you feel like a fraud.
- If you don't recognize yourself (you're not the same person you were two months ago).
- If it goes against your and your family's values and beliefs.
- If you follow the crowd or the general consensus.
- If you would just "die" if your parents saw you like this or doing this. The very thought makes you cringe.

## WHY DO SOME TEENS GIVE IN TO PEER PRESSURE?

Some kids succumb to peer pressure to fit in or be liked. If they don't fit in, other teens might tease them. Others follow out of curiosity. Even though they know better, if they believe "Everyone is doing it," they may follow suit.

## WHAT ARE THE DEFENSES AGAINST HARMFUL PEER PRESSURE?

Peer pressure can suck, especially if you feel guilty afterward. However, resisting doesn't make you an outsider. You'll gain self-confidence and loyal friends. Trust me. Even if it's just one or two people, the crowd you attract by being yourself and doing what's right will last a lifetime.

Here are some ways to stand firm against the influence of peer pressure (How to handle peer pressure, n.d.).

## PAY ATTENTION TO EMOTIONS

If there's something about a scenario that doesn't sit right with you, then it probably isn't a good idea. Although it seems like your peers are content in this situation, it may not be ideal for you.

## BE INSIGHTFUL

Whenever you're ready to enter a challenging environment, it's a good idea to consider how you'll react under a variety of conditions. You should plan ahead before saying or doing anything.

## SAY NO

There are moments when refusing someone's request feels terrible. In some cases, you might not wish to cause distress or shame to another person. However, "no" may be a powerful tool, especially for young women. Express your discomfort to the individual putting pressure on you.

## SET UP A CODEWORD WITH YOUR PARENTS

This is something you can share with your parents to help you get out of a jam and get the support you need. In order to get out of trouble, you can always contact or text your parents and tell them you need to be picked up or told to go home. It can be fun, too.

## FIND PEOPLE THAT SHARE YOUR VALUES AND WORLDVIEW

Hang out with people who have the same ideals. By mutually choosing to reject an option, you can reduce the complexity of a situation.

## TRY TO GET SOME HELP FROM AN OLDER PERSON

Choose someone you feel comfortable talking to, including a parent, teacher, or counselor, to help you escape peer pressure. A responsible adult is someone who can listen to your concerns and provide guidance on how to move forward.

## KNOW WHAT IS RIGHT

Trust your gut instincts when it comes to right and wrong. Is that the correct thing to do? Most likely, you already know the response. Knowing what is right helps you maintain your composure.

## HELP A FRIEND

Perhaps you notice that a friend has difficulty resisting peer pressure. Saying, "I'm with you; let's go," will be helpful.

## STEP ASIDE

There are still options available to you if peer pressure affects you while you're alone. Peers who push you to do things you know are wrong can be avoided. You can reply, "Nah. Not today," and then leave.

### DON'T BE A PEOPLE PLEASER

Keep in mind that you can't or shouldn't try to please or win over everyone. Accepting this can be challenging, but trying is helpful.

## Surrounding Yourself With the Right People

When you are around strangers, do you feel the same when you're around your best friend? I reckon not.

As humans, we attract each other and eventually adopt some of the qualities of people we spend a lot of time with. Think about it. Have you ever had a favorite phrase, and after a few months of hanging out, your bestie keeps saying the same thing too? In the same way, we exchange energy (positivity and negativity), ambitions, motives, and dreams.

So, it is crucial as young adults to surround ourselves with the right people.

### HOW TO MAKE FRIENDS

Perhaps making friends has never come easily to you, or maybe you recently moved and have no friends. Whatever the cause, keep in mind that everyone eventually needs to establish new friends, no matter the stage of life. So, here are a few tips to help you make friends.

### BE FRIENDLY

Although it may seem obvious, being nice is the first step in making friends. If you appear grumpy, negative, or distant, nobody will want to meet up with you. It can be intimidating to initiate a friendship, but breathe deeply and give it a shot.

### JUST SMILE

Smiling shows others how friendly you are. Even when you are anxious and in an unfamiliar situation, smiling makes you seem approachable to others. Smiling is contagious, so others will smile back at you.

### SAY HI

The truth is, some people will ignore you if you say hello, and it sucks, but you should be careful to pick the correct circumstance. Don't say hello to someone who is late for class or having an interesting chat on a Monday morning.

## ASK FOR HELP

Start a conversation by requesting assistance. Even if you already know the answer, ask about due dates for homework assignments to see if you can find a partner to work with. You'd be astonished at how happily individuals welcome the chance to assist.

## CONSTRUCT CONVERSATIONS

A conversation can be started in a variety of ways.

- During homeroom, introduce yourself and the topics of the day.
- Ask your classmate about a notice on the bulletin board or an announcement made yesterday.
- Inform someone giving you directions of your purpose before leaving.
- Discussing the food served in the school cafeteria always draws a lot of attention.
- Simply be yourself, go carefully, and avoid being overbearing.

## JOIN A CLUB

Participate in extracurricular activities at school. Join a group in which you actually have an interest. Your company will be like-minded if you do it that way.

## LOCAL RECREATIONAL AND VOLUNTEER ACTIVITIES

Look for local activities in newspapers, on bulletin boards, or by asking your teachers. This way, you can make friends away from school while doing something fun and engaging in the community. This is also an excellent way of building networks.

## TRY NEW THINGS WITH AN OPEN MIND

Trying out new interests or activities can help you meet new people as they bring you out and around.

## TRY TO MAINTAIN CONTACT

A good friend will be worth the time and effort it takes to make one. Maintaining a willingness to communicate will support the friendship. Additionally, you can use this to plan a meeting and do something together or to get to know them better.

## MAKING FRIENDS IF YOU'RE SHY

Shyness may indicate worries about who you are and how others see you, or you may have simply grown to be reserved. You may worry about making a social mistake, appearing dull and strange, or being ignored. Either way, fear of rejection prevents you from initiating friendships.

Here are some tips to help if you're shy:

- Avoid adding clever comments while entering a conversation. Everyone slips up once in a while, so always be a good listener. Simply smile, apologize, or crack a joke if that occurs to you. Keep in mind that it's likely nobody noticed.

- Don't worry about what other people think of you; most people are more interested in the image they are portraying than they are in judging your actions.

- Try to alter your perception of yourself by focusing on your positive qualities.

- Make travel plans with a friend if you are both attending the same event.

- Arrive early for a gathering or party so you can meet people as they arrive, and stay chill as more early-comers trickle in.

- Offer to help; being occupied will make you feel better.

- Plan a way out in case everything becomes too much for you. Say you might have to go early but that you'll remain as long as you can.

- Make an effort to connect with other shy people. Putting people at ease will benefit them, and it will also make you feel better about yourself.

- Don't simply join a group because it appears to be popular. Look for people you can relate to.

## TOXIC RELATIONSHIPS

Think about your life for a minute and the people who surround you. Think about their influence, how they make you feel, and what you don't like about them. In your vision, is there a friend who constantly gets on your last nerve, irritates you, and makes you uncomfortable? Maybe it's an old friend, and the friendship is too valuable to lose.

We all love our friends dearly, but sometimes that affection blinds us to the detrimental effects of their behavior. It's crucial to develop the ability to spot the signs of a toxic and mentally draining person for our own good.

If, after reflecting on your friendship, you notice any of the warning signs listed below, you should reconsider your connection with them. Warnings that your friend can be poisonous are given below (Adcock, 2021).

## THE FOCUS IS ON THEM AND THEIR ISSUES

These are the kinds of friends who might call and hog your time for an hour while venting, "checking in," and talking about themselves. When you have an issue and need a friend, they are nowhere to be found.

They Don't Care About You or Your Personal Space

Friends that don't respect boundaries are not friends at all. They might try to drag you to somewhere that you repeatedly insist upon NOT going to or take all of your clothing and jewelry while you're unaware.

## THEY TRY TO CHANGE YOU

When friends value and appreciate each other's individual characteristics, their friendship grows. Toxic friends, however, could try to influence you to behave in ways that aren't true to who you are. They could put you in awkward circumstances or demand that you change the way you speak, act, or dress.

## THERE IS ALWAYS TROUBLE

"Oh no, not again!" You might find yourself saying this over and over again when you're with them. If your friend always evokes problems, run.

## YOU'RE UNEASY AROUND THEM

You shouldn't feel nervous around a friend. If you are (even when you don't know why), then there is an issue. Simply being in the presence of a great friend should make you feel better.

## THEY ARE UNPREDICTABLE

Some people can be fun. Nonetheless, some friends lean toward the wild card group. If someone makes you feel threatened, under attack, or afraid, then you're not in a good friendship.

## THEY OFTEN TALK BADLY ABOUT OTHERS

Hearing unfavorable things about others can breed suspicion, even if your friend is the one with the information. You shouldn't confide in anybody who is always finding something to criticize in others. These people can't be trusted with your own secrets.

## THEY NEVER TAKE ACCOUNTABILITY

A toxic friend is "never wrong." However, respect for a friend means admitting our mistakes, apologizing, and trying to fix them. When confronted about their inappropriate behavior, toxic friends usually never apologize.

## THEY NEVER PAY ATTENTION TO YOU

In contrast, toxic friends aren't the kind who give you much support or praise. They won't lift you up; they'll bring you down.

## THEY'RE JEALOUS OF YOUR OTHER FRIENDS

Thinking you should only have one friend, which should only be them, is very much toxic. A toxic friend might even try to harm your other relationships with friends.

## YOUR CONNECTION IS CONDITIONAL

Like romantic partnerships, friends should adore you for who you are. Conditional friendships are damaging because they depend on you doing, wearing, or being something in a certain manner. This friend only supports you when they approve.

## THE FRIENDSHIP CAUSES WORRY TO OTHER FRIENDS OR FAMILY

Note if close friends, relatives, or trusted people express worry about a friendship. They care about you. If they observe a change in your behavior after being with this person, they may not want you to keep the friendship.

## YOU FEEL USED

Being generous in friendships is great, but it's easy to be exploited. A friend who only asks for money or favors is probably putting their needs before the friendship.

## FEELING COMPELLED TO BE THEIR FRIEND OR TRAPPED BY THEM

Some toxic friends resort to emotional abuse techniques to keep their friendships intact. Relationships that are emotionally abusive can feel chaotic and unsettling.

Typical indications of ongoing emotional abuse in friendships include the following:

- joking or threatening to harm themselves if you aren't there
- often criticizing you (and then leading you to believe that you're being unreasonable)
- acting differently in public versus privately while you two are together
- moving the blame around a lot to make it appear like you're the one who's at fault
- testing your devotion and allegiance frequently

## YOU CONTINUE TO LIE OR PROTECT THEM

Maybe others saw your friend's dubious actions. Maybe they've approached you to discuss something that's making them nervous or upset. If you want to defend or minimize their actions, pay attention. You may be enabling their misdeeds.

## OPTIONS TO DEAL WITH A TOXIC FRIENDSHIP

Toxic relationships are hard to fix and usually have two possibilities: fix or end it. Many pick the first option before breaking up, but there is no right or wrong way to proceed. Remember that inaction may worsen the problem.

## FIX IT

Prioritize what you can control. Consider your usual response to your friend, and add boundaries. Discuss the impact of your friendship with them. After seeing how your friend reacts, you can decide whether to end your friendship.

## END IT

You're free to end a friendship. Your toxic friend doesn't need an explanation. Consider a no-contact breakup. Remove them from your contacts, and stop texting and calling. No matter what, avoid talking.

*Segue: In this chapter, we focused on bettering yourself through building confidence, focusing on positive self-talk, not succumbing to peer pressure, and surrounding yourself with the right people. In the following chapter, we will take a look at caring for yourself—typically your outer self.*

# KNOW YOUR WORTH

During these times of constant social media interactions, it's hard not to compare ourself to others. The first step to self-confidence is recognizing your own awesome, unique qualities. In these mirrors, practice now by writing down at least three different things you love and appreciate about yourself, either inside or outside.

# Chapter 2: Personal Care and Listening to Your Changing Body

We were probably all excited for puberty—the "Big P" that paves the path to becoming a woman. It was supposed to be graceful and lovely; that is, until we found out the real truth: it can suck.

Boobs didn't just grow once overnight, and the sore tenderness that came with those two uneven buds didn't have a warning. We didn't realize that getting long legs would mean growing taller than some of the boys, including the cute guy from gym class. Ugh, so embarrassing! And not to mention bleeding once a month! Who came up with that?

It was more than you might've signed up for, and the worst part is that you have no control over it when it occurs. There are those mornings when you literally feel like a different person from the day before.

Did your body odor change so much that traditional deodorants stopped working? Someone "noticed?" Maybe your entire P.E. class made fun of your new "long" leg hair. Or when you raised your hand in class and armpit hair erupted out of nowhere.

You'll have puberty stories (the embarrassment gets better with time, trust me). But don't worry about the changes in your body—at least, don't panic.

In this chapter, we'll discuss some pointers for keeping up with your changing body, advice on maintaining your personal hygiene, and even a few fun things about growing up, like learning about makeup.

## Skincare

Self-care is the best care, and with it is one of its babies: skincare. Skincare, no matter what form or shape, is important, not to mention it boosts your confidence and takes you to another level of self-love. It's important that we take care of our skin, no matter how old we are or the color of our skin.

## SUNSCREEN

Most people know that sunscreen prevents sunburn and other injuries in the summer, but it should be used year-round. Wear sunscreen regardless of skin tone. Primers, foundations, serums, and creams contain water-resistant sunscreens.

### 4 REASONS YOU SHOULD USE SUNSCREEN

The top five reasons to wear sunscreen every day all year round are as follows:

- It guards your skin against UV rays.
- It reduces your risk of skin cancer.
- It stops the skin from aging prematurely.
- It supports a consistent skin tone.

### THE 4 W'S (AND H) OF SUNSCREEN

A proper sun protection plan should include SPF sunscreen. So, who should wear sunscreen, what can you actually use, at what time should you use it, and how?

These include the 4 W's and H of sunscreen, and they are discussed below:

- **Who:** Everyone (except for infants under six months old) should use sunscreen. To protect our skin, we should use some sort of sunscreen.
- **What:** Sunscreen comes in a variety of forms, including lotion, sprays, and sticks. None is inherently better than the other. Although lotions are more moisturizing than sprays, their shelf lives are likely to be shorter, and sprays are simple to use.
- **When:** Honestly, regardless of the season, we ought to wear it whenever we are outside.
- **Where:** Sunscreen is applied to your entire body, not only the parts that are exposed to the sun directly. Be sure to pay attention to the following frequently overlooked areas:
    - hairline
    - ears/neck

- feet, hands, and back
- **How:** For each application, apply one ounce (3 tablespoons) to the entire body. The two-finger rule is an SPF application technique in which you apply sunscreen to one area of your body, such as your face or neck, by squeezing it along the length of two fingers. Simply spritz just enough product to cover the area between the crease of your palm and the tips of your middle and index fingers, apply to an area of your body, and then repeat.

## SHAVING

Every girl has a different ideal time to shave, and contrary to popular belief, shaving doesn't cause the hair to grow thicker. Some girls start when their leg hair darkens, while others wait until it grows back completely. However, if it's your first time shaving, follow a checklist to avoid cuts and nicks.

Shaving appears easy. However, removing hair without bleeding requires skill. So, the right tools, advice, and patience help to make a fantastic leg-shaving experience.

### WHAT RAZOR SHOULD I USE WHEN SHAVING? (PROS AND CONS)

Although the lady commercials and razor packages make it look so easy, actually knowing how to shave is an entirely different story. Hence, it's okay to get help from an adult like a parent or elder sibling. But don't worry. Over time, you'll get better at shaving without nicking or scratching yourself (WebMD, 2022.).

Choose a razor that won't cut you while yet doing the job. There are both electric and manual razors available.

The following are some specifics regarding each kind of razor:

### ELECTRIC RAZORS

To get rid of unwanted hair, many people turn to electric razors. They are available in a variety of cordless, battery-powered, and rechargeable forms. Go with a razor designed for teens.

### SAFETY OR DISPOSABLE RAZORS

Shaving cream or gel may be needed if you use a safety razor or disposable razor. They help in the healing process of cuts and scrapes. Don't use any gels or lotions that include alcohol, as this can be quite irritating to the skin.

Manual razors, on the other hand, cut beneath the skin's surface to provide a more delicate shave.

## HOW TO START ANY SHAVING ROUTINE

Investing in quality shaving equipment is crucial, at least for the first few times you shave. This will help you learn what constitutes a decent shave.

The following tools are required to shave:

- an exfoliator
- moisturizing shaving cream
- blade of outstanding quality
- moisturizer

While additional items, such as a skin brush, pre-shave oil, and others, can be utilized, you will be shaving like an expert in no time with these high-quality tools.

Follow these five steps to get a nice, clean shave:

1. Ensure that the skin is prepared.
2. Never forget the shaving cream.
3. Shave along the growth direction of your hair.
4. Use a moisturizer.
5. Don't forget to dry the razor.

## HOW TO SHAVE THE DIFFERENT PARTS OF YOUR BODY

Here is where we get to the really important part: the actual shaving. Since each body part is unique, the following is a useful guide:

- **Legs:** Shave softly upwards as far as your little heart wishes, beginning at the ankles. Reapply gel as desired or as necessary.
- **Armpits:** After using your gel or mousse in this area, you are free to shave in any direction you like—downward, upward, sideways, diagonally, and so on.

- **Bikini region:** Exfoliate first to remove dirt and dead skin. This reduces shaving ingrown hairs. Shave in the direction of the line of the hair growth after applying gel or mousse. To keep things smooth, reapply and shave backward against hair growth.

- **Facial hair:** Let's get straight to the point since nobody knows you are reading this: It grows on your face. And sometimes, it's difficult to control, even if there are only a few wayward wisps. So shaving away a mustache is okay. And no, it doesn't get any thicker when it grows back. If you pluck or thread your eyebrows and you prefer this method to retain the perfect shape, stick with it.

## WHAT TO DO IF YOU GET A CUT OR A NICK

Avoid cuts when shaving thighs or underarms. But if you do get a cut, wash and dry the wound.

If you cut yourself shaving your pubic hair, bathe with soft soap and water and pat dry. Next time, try an electric razor. Contact your doctor if symptoms continue.

The home remedies listed below are more effective and less humiliating for treating cuts and nicks from shaving:

- **Hot compress or hot water:** By helping to singe the wound, placing a hot compress or cloth on the cut or running hot water directly on it can stop the bleeding.

- **Ice water:** Blood vessels will constrict when you splash cold water on your face or even apply an ice cube to a larger cut.

- **Vaseline:** Applying lip balm or even Vaseline to a wound will aid in sealing the skin around the cut. Don't forget to apply lip balm to your injury using a cotton swab.

- **Witch hazel:** Witch hazel has anti-inflammatory properties. As an astringent, witch hazel will tighten blood vessels to reduce or stop bleeding.

- **Sugar:** This will aid in stopping the bleeding but, more significantly, will help to clean up the wound and get rid of any harmful bacteria.

- **Eye drops:** By tightening blood vessels, applying a few drops to a nick or cut will reduce bleeding time.

# Basic Grooming

Looking and feeling your best is a top objective in your teenage years. Being up to standard with your skin, hygiene, and hair care can help you achieve this.

For this reason, it's critical to start using effective hair care methods and procedures at a young age to guarantee that your hair is strong and fabulously lustrous and your nails are clean and beautiful.

## HAIR CARE TIPS

The truth is, your hair may break or grow more slowly if you ignore it. The good news is that there is still time to take care of it and get it healthy again. You can simply use ordinary routines instead of pricey hair products.

Here are some hair care tips for all hair types.

## CARE ADVICE FOR DRY HAIR

Dry hair feels crunchy and fragile. Certain treatments and genetics can cause dry hair. Dry hair should be washed less often, and check the brand to ensure your shampoo and conditioner replenishes essential oils. Look for "hydrating" and "moisturizing" on hair care labels.

Heat and chemicals can damage dry hair.

Despite their popularity, electric hair straighteners, dryers, and curlers damage hair. Use these heated tools less often to keep your hair healthy (or at least in a less hot setting).

Finally, take extra precautions while it's sunny outside. Sunlight and chlorine dry out hair. Wearing a helmet or avoiding the sun is the easiest way to protect your hair.

## CARE ADVICE FOR OILY HAIR

An oily scalp causes oily hair. Perhaps you should try applying the shampoo to your head for at least 5 minutes before rinsing, and simply condition the ends of your hair (avoid the scalp).

Additionally, oily hair benefits from a little talcum powder at the roots.

## CARING FOR CURLY HAIR

Here are some tips to help you care for and style jaw-dropping curls:

## WASHING PROCESS

- Use a shampoo that is nourishing and moisturizing.
- Pick sulfate-free products instead! Sulfates can remove your hair's natural oils.
- Don't wash too much.
- It's sufficient to do this twice per week.
- Never leave the hair conditioner behind.

## STYLE ADVICE

- Try a blow dryer with a diffuser attachment to ensure that your coils are ideal and frizz-free.
- After shampooing, don't forget the curl cream or serum.
- A wide-toothed comb can be used to untangle the knots.

## PRODUCT INGREDIENTS

Hair care depends on products. Natural products are preferable, so check the ingredients before buying. If the first five ingredients are words you can't pronounce, it probably contains chemicals and fragrances and isn't for you. Instead, check for these ingredients (some aren't listed below but are just as great):

- Argan oil
- Burdock root
- Castor oil
- Jojoba oil & Esters
- Vitamin C and E oil

## MANAGING SPLIT ENDS

Split ends are visible if you look carefully. At the end of the thread, you can see a strand of hair that has actually split in half.

Heat, blow-drying, and brushing can cause split ends. Split ends must be trimmed in a salon. However, avoiding extreme heat and cold, combing less, using conditioner, and covering your hair can prevent split ends.

## SIX TIPS FOR MAINTAINING HEALTHY HAIR

Overall, your hair is dependent on how you treat it, and what works for me might not work for you. So, here are six general tips to take care of your hair no matter the texture or length:

- Accept your hair as it is. Fighting nature damages hair more.
- Get your hair checked out on a regular basis.
- Know what you are using.
- Frequent brushing can split and break your hair, despite its shiny appearance. So, do it sparingly.
- Leave color changes to the experts.
- When braiding hair, use caution.
- Maintain a nutrient-rich diet.
- Stay away from really hot water.

## TRIMMING YOUR NAILS

A straightforward yet crucial self-care practice is nail grooming. Short, well-kept nails look great and are less likely to gather dirt and bacteria. Nail clipping can also prevent hangnails and ingrown toenails.

Despite its simplicity, nail clipping requires numerous steps to ensure a good trim.

The following advice is for proper nail trimming:

- **Soften nail:** Following a bath or shower is the ideal time to trim your nails. If that isn't possible, you can soften your nails by soaking them in lukewarm water for a couple of minutes.
- **Use the necessary tools:** Use a toenail cutter for your toenails and a nail clipper or fingernail clippers for your fingernails. Do not forget to disinfect your instruments.
- **Cut nearly straight across the nail:** To keep nails strong and safe from clothing and furniture, round the corners using a nail file. To avoid in-

grown toenails, trim them straight across. Toenails grow more slowly than fingernails; thus, they may need less cutting.

- **Do not touch your cuticles:** It's vital to avoid cutting or pushing back your cuticles since they protect the nail root.
- **After trimming, moisturize to keep your nails flexible:** This is crucial because dry air makes it easier for nails to crack.

Your overall health is reflected in your nails. Consult a board-certified dermatologist if you observe a change in the tone, texture, or form of your nails.

# Makeup

Before we go any further, it's important to understand that makeup isn't a necessity, and you shouldn't feel pressured to wear it if you really don't want to. It is natural to feel the need to fit in and meet the "standards" that social media sets, but your natural skin is beautiful with or without makeup, and it should only be used if you feel comfortable, if you have permission from parents, and if it simply makes you feel bolder (not prettier).

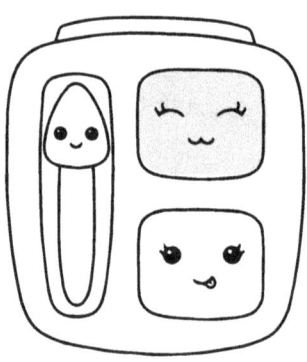

There are, however, a few negative impacts of makeup, which we will discuss first before getting into how it is actually used.

## DISADVANTAGES OF MAKEUP

Although wearing makeup is typically thought of as making you look attractive, did you know there are actually a lot of situations where you should avoid doing so? You can still look gorgeous by embracing your inner and natural beauty. However, many think makeup is the only way to look good.

But here are some surprising arguments against makeup, especially for acne-prone skin:

- It may result in allergic reactions.
- Instead of correcting flaws, you are covering them up.
- Products may contain chemicals that can cause or worsen acne.
- It takes up far too much time.

## BASIC MAKEUP ITEMS

Every day, we see cosmetic items and techniques. However, many beginners might still have trouble understanding how to apply makeup and what kind of makeup a teenage girl should wear.

Here are some teen makeup items and how to achieve a simple natural makeup look.

### PRIMER

If you have oily skin and want your foundation to last, start with a primer. Only apply it to the greasy parts of your face.

### FOUNDATION

Watery foundations provide covering. SPF-protected ones are also available. Apply the foundation only where you need protection and blend it for a natural look. Blend with your fingers—apply a bit at a time and build up. Beauty blenders create a flawless, natural look.

### CONCEALER

Concealers may hide flaws and dark circles without foundation. Blend concealer with your fingers, a medium-sized blending brush, or a small beauty blender.

### COSMETIC BROW GEL

Tinted brow gel is the easiest way to shape and thicken your brows.

### CREAM BLUSH

Cream blush is easy to apply and mixes well. It gives the cheeks and skin a healthy, natural shine. If you have acne, choose a light-pigmented powder blush that's easy to blend.

### CREAM HIGHLIGHTER

Cream highlighters blend well and are less sparkling and shiny, making them ideal for a natural look. Thus, it makes the skin glow.

### BUTTERY EYESHADOW

Cream eyeshadows only last for one use. You can apply and blend eyeshadow using just your finger, creating a look that is simple to achieve yet attractive and refined.

## EYELASHES

For a natural look, practice using an eyelash curler. To avoid pulling out eyelashes, get help and buy a nice one. For doe-eyed cuteness, use a lengthening, fluttery mascara. To lengthen and thicken lashes, apply castor oil before night.

## LIP STAINS

Lip stains are perfect for all-day wear.

## LIQUID LIPSTICK

If you like strong colors but want something simple that lasts all day, liquid lipsticks are long-lasting.

## LIP GLOSS

For moisturized lips, lip glosses are very popular. Reapply whenever you want.

## MAKEUP TIPS FOR BEGINNERS

Clear skin is essential and highly desired. You don't want to depend on foundation since you can't stop breakouts. Thus, follow this makeup process:

- Every night, wash with a mild cleanser.
- Tone after washing.
- Use oil sheets all day long, starting in the morning.
- Purchase a quality moisturizer with SPF.
- Try using concealer rather than foundation.
- Apply mascara on upper lashes.
- Choose your best feature and improve it.
- Regularly clean your makeup tools.
- Don't overdo your foundation.

## Tackling Unpleasant Odors

No one likes that yucky smell after running all day or facing that awful smell after eating seafood. But, especially as teens, you can be more prone to these unpleasant odors.

Not to worry, though. In this section, we'll look at how to efficiently tackle these odors and control them going forward.

## BAD BREATH

Most people have had bad breath before. It may be caused by a previous meal or a major health issue like cavities, gum disease, or acid reflux. Whatever the reason, it's an uncomfortable social situation and a hygienic issue.

Here are some ways to control bad breath:

- Gargle apple cider vinegar.
- Fresh parsley or mint leaves can reduce bad breath.
- Take care of your tongue.
- Keep hydrated.
- Natural toothbrushes are fibrous foods (apples, sugar-free gum, carrots).
- Consume foods that neutralize acid, like yogurt.
- Avoid being affected by coffee breath.
- Use lemon juice to rinse.

## BODY ODOR

All of us have been there. Your nose wrinkles when you catch a brief whiff of body odor, and then you have the horrible realization that it is coming from you.

These tips will help you maintain a fresh smell throughout the day:

- Take a shower or a bath each day.
- Make sure to wear clean clothes and wash your clothes frequently.
- Avoid eating foods with strong scents (like a lot of garlic) because they might permeate your skin.
- Apply antiperspirant before going to sleep.
- Dry off your underarms.
- Use a hydrogen peroxide and water mix. One cup (eight ounces) of water and one teaspoon of peroxide should do the trick.

- Deodorant is ideal for you.

- Stinky feet aren't cool. Wet your shoes with pure isopropyl alcohol (rubbing alcohol) using a spray bottle.

- Spike the laundry. Use up to one cup of washing soda or baking soda to eliminate odors. Before washing, use a bucket or your washing machine's "soak" option.

- Before washing them, turn your clothing inside out.

- Avoid using the dryer on any technical fabrics or really stinky clothing.

- What you eat, you sweat.

- Speak to your doctor if you experience excessive sweating.

## How To Shop for a Bra

Making memories and adjusting to numerous changes are important aspects of being a girl that will help shape the woman you will become in the future. When you discover some truly spectacular and somewhat awkwardly felt bodily changes, there should be two key moments: first, the start of periods, and second, the day you put on your very first bra!

In this section, we cover everything you need to think about when deciding how to purchase a bra.

### FINDING THE CORRECT BRA

There are countless options for bra styles. There are push-up bras, training bras, sports bras, soft-cup bras, underwired bras, and more. Which is the best for you?

What level of support is required should be taken into account when choosing the appropriate type of bra. Do you require extra support while playing sports, or do you only need enough to cover up while you're developing? Or perhaps you already have an underwire since you have larger breasts?

Here are a few types to consider.

### TRAINING BRAS

Training bras are soft bras that provide support, covering, and comfort. Perfect for first-time budders.

## SPORTS BRAS

Sports bras support delicate breast tissue during exercise.

## SOFT CUP BRAS

If you want a supportive bra that looks natural, a soft cup bra, or bralette, is a great choice. Without wires, these bras support breasts without raising, shaping, or squeezing them.

## UNWIRED BRAS

Wired or non-wired bras are largely dependent on comfort. Not everyone likes wired bras. Some girls dislike wires, while others adore the support. Underwired bras with U-shaped wires at the bottom of each cup support breasts in women with C-cups or larger.

## GETTING THE RIGHT MEASUREMENTS

Bra shopping shouldn't be stressful. Try on many styles before choosing. Be careful and ensure you are comfortable because a poorly fitted bra can also lead to migraines, back issues, and muscle pain.

Here are a few things to consider about your bra sizes.

## BAND SIZE

You only need a measuring tape to determine the band size, which you can do either at home or in a store. Completely deflate your chest, then measure the area beneath the bust by encircling it with a measuring tape. To the nearest full number, write it down.

## BUST SIZE

Put the measuring tape around you and across your nipple to determine your bust size.

## CUP SIZE

Now that you know your band size and breast size, just figure out how they differ from one another. You have an AA-cup if the difference is less than half an inch; if it is between half and one inch, you have an A-cup.

You have a B-cup if the difference is between one and two inches and a C-cup if it is between two and three inches. Three to four inches have D-cups, whereas five inches or more have DD or E-cups.

## PERFECT FITTING BRA

If you face any of the following issues after you have chosen a bra, then you have chosen the wrong one:

- back and neck issues
- breast ache
- nipple ache
- skin problems
- headaches

## UNDERBAND ISSUES

Since the bulk of the support comes from the underband, it is crucial to get the size right. You should either get a new bra or a smaller size if your band rolls up from front to back.

- **Chafing:** Using sports bras causes chafing for many girls. Chafing can happen when the skin and the cloth move or come into contact with each other. Consider going down a size for a closer fit.

- **The bottom of the boob popping out:** Some girls might observe that their boobs protrude from under their bras. Another indication that your underband is slack is that it doesn't fit snugly against your skin. Check if your cup size is adequate, and think about going down a size in your underband.

## CUP ISSUES

- **The 4 boob look:** If you are bulging out of your cup, it's probably too tiny, and you should size up.

- **Side boob:** If you are popping out the side, size bigger.

- **Boobs are not seated flush:** Your bra's cups are too small if you experience gapping at the front center and should think about going up a size.

- **Underwires digging in:** Your breast flesh must be completely enclosed by the bra's underwire. It's possible that your bra is the wrong size for you and doesn't fit you properly if the wires in it are uncomfortable for you.

- **Excess fabric:** You should size down a cup size if you discover that there is extra material in your cup.

- **Not filling the cup:** Consider scaling down a cup size if, while wearing the bra, you can see the interior of the cup.

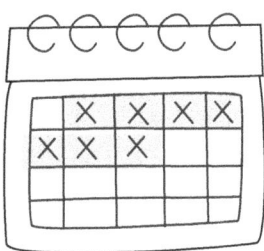

## All About Your Period

Whether you have already gotten it or not, your period is another "right of passage" that can seem exciting at first but usually becomes something like a menace every month. Either way, it's a natural thing that your body has to go through, so it's important to understand everything that it comes with and how to care for yourself throughout it. So, now we'll take a look at what to expect from your period and how to deal with it every month.

### WHAT'S YOUR PERIOD?

In blunt and simple terms, a girl's uterus releases blood through her vagina during her menstruation. Your period usually indicates that you are at the peak of puberty and, in a few years, will be completely done with it.

### PMS

Premenstrual syndrome (PMS) causes mental and physical problems in girls before and during their periods. These symptoms include mood changes, anxiety, bloating, acne, and irritability. Symptoms disappear after a few days.

### HOW CAN I TELL WHEN MY PERIOD IS DUE?

As periods approach, some females experience bloating, acne, aching breasts, and emotional instability. Back, leg, and stomach cramps may occur before your period starts. Not everyone can predict their period, and symptoms can vary from month to month. Growing makes period prediction easier.

Tracking your periods can help determine when your next period will start. It may also reveal your cycle time. Teens often have irregular periods.

## CAN I CONCEIVE RIGHT AFTER MY PERIOD STARTS?

Yes, as soon as your period begins, you can become pregnant. The reason for this is that your hormones may already be in motion. Even if you have never had a period, you can still become pregnant if you have sex.

## HOW LONG DOES IT LAST?

The average period lasts five days. A cycle, however, might be either shorter or longer.

## HOW FREQUENTLY DOES A PERIOD OCCUR?

Usually, a period occurs every 4-5 weeks. However, some girls experience a bit less or more frequent cycles.

## HOW MUCH BLOOD LEAVES?

Even though it appears to be a lot of blood, you typically only shed a few tablespoons of blood throughout your entire period.

## WILL I CONTINUE TO EXPERIENCE PERIODS?

Women's periods will permanently end when they reach menopause (approximately age 45 to 55). Additionally, women who are pregnant won't have periods.

## HOW TO MANAGE YOUR PERIOD

The following menstrual products are made to absorb menstrual blood, so you don't have to stress about leaks or stains on your clothes while you're out and about.

## PADS

These small patches of absorbent material called pads are attached to your undergarments. Pads are available in a wide range of sizes and levels of absorbency. Pads with wings are another option.

There are two different types of pads that do the same task but are applied slightly differently.

- Disposable pads: Sticky strips are on the bottom of most pads. After removing the paper strip covering the adhesive, you then put the pad in your underwear. The pad's wings (if there are any) should be wrapped around the crotch.

When removing it, unstick the pad from your underwear, then wrap it in toilet paper. Place it in the trash bin or the special disposal box in restroom stalls. Pads can block toilets, so don't flush them.

- Reusable pads: Wearing these pads requires washing. These pads are fastened to underwear and are cheaper and greener.

## TAMPONS

Since tampons are absorbent and thin, they are placed in the vagina to absorb blood. Tampons have different levels of absorbency, like pads. Despite their frightening appearance, tampons are simple to use.

Most tampons feature applicators for easy insertion. Use a portable mirror for your first tampon. Remove it after 3–4 hours. Prolonged tampon use can cause Toxic Shock Syndrome (TSS), a rare but dangerous bacterial infection. To avoid blocking drains and toilets, wrap tampons with toilet paper before discarding them in the provided bin.

## HOW ARE TAMPONS USED?

You can use your finger or applicator to insert a tampon. Use the right tampon and change it every few hours.

Tampon strings should remain out. Remove the tampon gently, wrap it in toilet paper, and dispose of it. Never flush tampons. Tampons aren't visible like pads; therefore, you must remember to change them.

Don't panic if you can't find the string to change your tampon. Simply reach in and pull the string. It might take a minute since the string can be hard to hold.

## MENSTRUAL CUPS

Reusable menstrual cups collect blood. Most are silicone. Menstrual cups can be used for 6–12 hours, depending on flow. The cup can be taken out, drained, cleaned, and then reinserted.

## MENSTRUAL DISKS

These are disposable menstrual discs, not cups. Usually, medical-grade polymers make them. Menstrual discs function similarly to cups by catching your flow. However, placement, shape, and insertion vary.

Pinch the disc to insert it. When inserting, push it back till the top of the rim touches your pubic bone. Muscular walls support menstrual discs.

## PERIOD PANTIES

Some period panties can replace pads or menstrual cups, while others are for added protection. Instead of disposable menstrual products, period panties are eco-friendly. Period panties must be cleaned and maintained after each use.

## HOW DO I CHOOSE WHAT TO EMPLOY?

Choose your period protection. Some girls prefer tampons because they're portable. Swimmers can use tampons and cups as pads are banned in water.

Pads are convenient and simple to change. Some women with regular leaking also use tampons as well as pads.

A lot of girls choose based on

- their predicament
- where they'll be located
- their monthly period
- period of time (day or night coverage)

## PRODUCTS TO RELIEVE MENSTRUAL PAIN

Periods sometimes hurt. Menstrual cramps, which cause lower abdominal pain, are the most common period discomfort. Headaches, nausea, and lower back pain are among other issues. These things may reduce menstruation pain:

- Midol
- heat treatment
- electrical nerve stimulator
- hormonal birth control
- stress reduction

## QUICK PERIOD HACKS

Feeling blah (often pronounced TERRIBLE) and having periods seem to go with each other. Bloating, pains, bleeding, and the all-too-common emotional ups and downs brought on by hormone malfunctions are just a few of the things your body deals with.

However, here are a few tricks to survive the horrific week of your period with as minimal discomfort as possible.

## GETTING RID OF PERIOD PAIN

Do your thighs, lower back, or lower abdomen feel tight? If the answer is yes, you are probably dealing with menstrual cramps. Menstrual cramps might start one or two days before your period and last several days. Some girls have minimal symptoms, while others have severe headaches, dizziness, nausea, and loose stools.

To relieve mild period cramps, you can:

- Apply a heating pad to your lower back or stomach.
- Take a hot bath.
- Apply a hot water bottle to your lower back or stomach.
- Take over-the-counter painkillers or anti-inflammatory medication (after consulting a doctor).
- Engage in a simple workout like yoga, walking, or swimming.

## REDUCE BLOATING

The period bloat is a typical symptom that you may experience before and during your period. It may make your stomach feel tight. There are ways to reduce bloating, but no treatment is perfect.

- Your ally is water.
- Eat wholesome foods.
- Reduce caffeine.
- Engage in physical activity.
- Get lots of Zs.

## COMBATING ODOR

Vaginal odor is naturally sour or sweet. During your menstruation and ovulation, your vagina is delicately acidic. Lactobacilli help maintain equilibrium, so mild vaginal odors that might smell like bread, for example, may be okay.

Is it stinky? That's okay! The crotch contains many sweat glands, so sometimes your smell is surprising. Simply clean your groin. Instead of soap, rinse your vulva with warm water.

Yeast infections cause itching, burning, and white cottage cheese-like discharge with a strong fishy or yeasty smell. They are common and treatable infections. Ask your doctor about a one-time therapy or buy an antifungal suppository or lotion from the pharmacy.

## OUTFIT IDEAS TO STAY COMFORTABLE DURING YOUR PERIOD

Many of us experience our periods once a month. When we are menstruating, things are difficult, so we're using our clothing (along with warm stomach tea) to help make things a little bit easier. When getting dressed during your period, the goal is to feel confident in your appearance, even though your body may be experiencing physical fatigue.

So how do we handle those challenging few days each month? Here are some outfits you might want to consider:

- loose materials
- thicker materials (e.g., sweats)
- large t-shirt
- darker shades

## PROBLEMS TO WATCH OUT FOR

Everything from lifestyle elements like stress and exercise habits to underlying medical issues like a bleeding disorder or hormone imbalances can contribute to irregular periods. Although it might not be clear right away if you have atypical periods because it might take some time for the menstruation to regulate, there are certain warning signals you can look out for.

If you see any of the following, make an appointment to see a doctor (De Jong & Pradhan, 2022):

- being 15 years old and not having a period
- irregular cycles that last more than two years following the start of your period

- strong cramping that doesn't go away with painkillers or very heavy bleeding (bleeding through a pad or tampon in an hour or less)
- bleeding for more than a week
- having significant PMS symptoms

Although these symptoms may not necessarily mean something is wrong, it's a good idea to consult a healthcare professional just to be safe.

It all can be scary and sometimes frustrating, but doing the right things for your health and comfort will never lead you astray.

*Segue: In this chapter, we looked at some basic personal skills that teenage girls can employ to take care of themselves, including skincare, grooming, beauty, hygiene, simple teenage rights of passage, and having a period. In the following chapter, we will dive into the world of politeness.*

# YOUR CHANGING BODY

The changes to our bodies happens differently for everyone, and many of them can be awkward. We gave you some tips on improving and finding ways to deal with these changes, but the first step is to acknowledge them. What are some ways you've found your own body to be changing?

# Chapter 3: The Power of Politeness

## Manners are the traffic lights for life.
### —Dr. P. M. Forni

— ♥ — ▲ — ♥ — ▲ — ♥ —

Do we still have time to think about manners in our quick-paced world, when divorce rates, drug and alcohol abuse, and violence are on the rise, in addition to the apparently never-ending problems?

Proper manners are lacking in today's society, although many of us learn how to be courteous as children. We are taught how to be kind to other people and animals, how to respect our elders, and how to say please and thank you.

It's crucial to recognize and value good manners. Therefore, in this chapter, we will focus on the importance of good manners and how we can be polite as a foundation for our growth to adulthood.

## The Importance of Good Manners

Some could argue that using good manners these days is unfashionable.

But in truth, having good manners is essential for success in a variety of endeavors, partly because of the advantages they bring from childhood through adulthood. They can boost our confidence, improve our relationships, help us succeed, and improve our overall well-being. Good manners require respect for self and others. They'll enhance your life and those around you.

It's also good to note that it's free. Being polite and courteous, such as saying please and thank you, paying attention when others are speaking, and making eye contact, may have a positive impact on us and others.

Here are a few ways good manners can be beneficial.

### ENCOURAGES CONFIDENCE

We build our confidence by deciding what to do in any given situation and then really doing it. Additionally, it guards against humiliation as a result of a careless statement or improper behavior.

## THE BEST IMPRESSION POSSIBLE

First impressions matter. They lay the foundation for upcoming connections and chances. When you meet a stranger, they are completely unfamiliar to you. Naturally, people draw conclusions about you based on your appearance, behavior, and conversation.

Meeting someone for the first time might be frightening, but being polite lessens the pressure, and you never know where a great first impression will lead you.

## OPENS THE DOOR TO OPPORTUNITIES

Even the best school cannot open all the doors. The unplanned, possibly life-changing chances made possible by having good manners are one of the numerous advantages of having them.

Therefore, when an opportunity arises, a considerate, well-behaved person is frequently considered and requested.

## DEVELOPS COMPASSION FOR OTHERS

Visualize good manners in action. They resemble

- opening doors for other people
- giving support
- closing your mouth while chewing
- maintaining eye contact

From this point, it is obvious that smart action has positive effects on society in addition to oneself.

## PROTECTIONS AGAINST SELFISHNESS

Selfishness wrecks reputations and breaks relationships. However, good manners naturally defend against this condition. You can't live a well-mannered life without considering how your actions influence other people unless you "fake it," of course.

## EMBRACES JOY

The satisfaction of helping others is immense. Knowing that your behavior and mannerisms benefit those around you gives you a deep sense of satisfaction. Even though it seems like no one is seeing your good behavior, you can still feel proud of yourself (but rest assured they do).

## ENCOURAGES REPLICATION

When others are kind to us, it's simple for us to return the favor. It's that simple, and in the same way, when you are courteous to someone, they are more likely to help when you need it. When someone shares with us, we are more inclined to reciprocate.

Therefore, even if we are not motivated by reciprocation, it is a very appealing benefit.

## BUILDS THE FOUNDATION FOR LIFE SUCCESS

To succeed in life, you need more than just a lot of effort. Together, hard work and excellent manners make a powerful team that can overcome any challenge. Beyond the dining table, proper manners are admirable, and people respect things they admire.

## ENHANCES INTERPERSONAL RELATIONS

Who are the types of people you are looking to be friends with? They most likely wouldn't be rude, self-serving, loudmouthed, or otherwise disagreeable people. It's human nature to gravitate toward those who are courteous, kind, and considerate of others.

## MAKES OTHER PEOPLE FEEL NOTICED AND VALUED

Good manners encourage people to be their best while showcasing their best qualities. A happier life can be had by consistently using these manners:

- being open
- being considerate
- being upbeat
- being kind
- being cooperative

- being helpful
- being impolite
- being respectful of others' privacy

People without manners are an outcast in society because they are unable to win others over. They might be a decent person, a great fighter, and intelligent, but they'll find it difficult to gain the respect of others if they lack manners.

## Social Etiquette

We might not all be social, but as we grow older, we'll soon realize that we actually need to know how to interact on a daily basis in order to survive, gain respect, and get by on a day-to-day basis. So, this section is designed to help you learn how to be sociable in the right way.

### HOW TO SHAKE HANDS

If you're meeting a friend, give them a firm handshake to help establish the tone of your chat. Here are a few tips on when to shake hands and how to do so in a polished, professional manner.

### TIMING OF HANDSHAKES

Avoid the uncomfortable situation of thinking about whether to shake or not. Just confidently extend your right hand! A firm handshake is always an excellent first impression.

The following circumstances call for a firm handshake:

- a first encounter with a stranger
- first encounter with the interviewer at a face-to-face job interview
- when you run into someone you haven't seen in a while
- whenever a hand is extended

### THE FIVE ELEMENTS OF A GOOD HANDSHAKE

First of all, when shaking hands, ensure that there are no weak handshakes or tight grips. One conveys your lack of confidence, while the other just intimidates others. You should have a secure and relaxed grasp.

Here are the five elements of a good handshake:

- The hinge is at your elbow, meaning your elbow shakes, not your wrist or shoulder.
- Your right hand is extended. To the other individual, you should be parallel.
- Eye contact is necessary for handshakes. Add your smile while maintaining eye contact with the other individual.
- Only 2 or 3 "shakes" constitute a handshake. Don't shake hands endlessly—1-2-3 and let the hands go.
- When shaking hands, always stand. Standing demonstrates respect for the person you are meeting and greeting, as well as your genuine interest in them.

## STRATEGIES FOR IMPROVING YOUR BUSINESS HANDSHAKE

Don't overthink it. There are other ways to communicate confidence and friendliness besides shaking hands.

Here are six suggestions for perfecting your handshake.

### UNDERSTAND WHEN TO REACH OUT A HAND

Frequently, the senior individual will initiate the handshake. Allow the senior management to extend their hand first when you are meeting them for the first time.

If you start the handshake, keep your palm up. If you extend your hand with your palm down, it may appear threatening.

### PROVIDE SINCERITY

To express how you feel about the interaction, think about making eye contact with the person and giving a genuine smile or other engaged response.

### TRY THE WEB

Go for the web on the other person's hand when extending your hand to shake. The action creates a palm-to-palm contact that enables you to firmly shake their hand.

## MODERATE THE PRESSURE

Avoid squeezing or pinching the other person's palms. The perfect handshake will be relaxed and match the other person's grasp pressure.

## KEEP IT SHORT

It takes two to four seconds to shake hands. If you initiated the handshake, attempt to break it off after three seconds to avoid upsetting the other person. Don't clean your hands after releasing your hold; doing so can be seen as offensive.

## ONCE MORE BEFORE YOU GO

Before leaving, if you've had a lengthy talk with the person, such as during an interview, shake hands with them.

# HOW TO INTRODUCE YOURSELF

New friends will enjoy and remember a strong self-introduction. Introducing yourself strongly is important to make a good impression.

Here are some tips for good self-introductions.

## MAKE IT RELEVANT

Pizza may be your favorite food, but unless you're a chef or attending a cooking class, it will feel cute and random. Be aware of the surroundings.

## BE UNIQUE

This does not imply that you must create a self-introduction essay if you are a writer. Just go the extra mile and elaborate a little bit more on the specifics of who you are.

## PREPARE

After introducing yourself to someone, ask yourself what you want to be known for, and then prepare for it.

## CONSIDER THE CULTURAL SETTING

If you're introducing yourself to a large audience, make sure not to upset anybody.

## BE MINDFUL WITH HUMOR

While humor is wonderful, refrain from telling jokes only for the sake of telling them. What you consider hilarious may not connect with others.

## HOW TO INTRODUCE YOURSELF IN A JOB INTERVIEW

Let's simply stick to the fundamentals here as we focus on how to respond to "tell me about yourself" questions. It's perhaps the most important part of an interview, so let's have it down solid.

### DO YOUR RESEARCH

To introduce yourself in the best possible manner, find out as much as you can about the firm you're applying to. Ensure that you suit the culture. This will help you to come up with the best answer to "What are you passionate about?" which should align with the company (wink, wink).

### BE MINDFUL OF YOUR BODY LANGUAGE

More than you may realize, body language conveys a lot of information. When introducing yourself to the hiring manager, you should

- Retain eye contact.
- Ensure your handshake is solid but not forced.
- Speak confidently.
- Avoid moving around, twitching, or crossing your arms.

## HOW TO INTRODUCE YOURSELF TO A RECRUITER IN AN EMAIL

Just think about it. When you enter the working world, you must actually land a job before you can even introduce yourself in a job interview.

Nowadays, the best approach to submitting a job application is via email. A strong introduction includes more than just one sentence or paragraph. The complete message is what matters.

Here are some tips to ensure you get it right.

### INCLUDE EVERY ASPECT OF AN EMAIL

Check to make sure your message begins with a subject line and concludes with your name. You can't leave anything out of your "introduce yourself" email.

## CREATE A COMPELLING SUBJECT LINE

The last thing you want to happen when you send an email introduction is to end up in the spam folder. Create a compelling subject line. When responding to a job offer, use the appropriate subject format.

## PICK A SUITABLE SALUTATION

"Dear Sir or Madam" appears careless in an email greeting. It implies that you are ignorant about your recipient. Try to address your Dear Sir or Dear Madam by name. If you don't know their names, do some digging.

## MAKE A STRONG INTRODUCTION

Give the background. Why are you writing this?

The key is relevancy. A message that doesn't strike a chord with the receiver will be immediately filed in the trash.

## MAKE YOUR PROPOSAL

Ask for an interview, then explain to the recruiting manager how you will help them. The most crucial element of your entire professional introduction is this.

## GRATITUDE IS DUE

Gratitude at the end of your email can increase the likelihood that you'll hear back from the recipient.

## TIPS FOR INTRODUCING OTHERS

The following are some common pointers to keep in mind when introducing other people to each other:

- Make sure you are aware of who you are introducing and to whom.

- Typically, you want to show the most regard or respect to the individual you select to make the introduction.

- Make eye contact with the person you are speaking to first, then while you are finishing the introduction, spin around and do the same with the other person.

- Speak clearly and slowly. The individuals you are introducing will find it simpler to learn and remember each other's names as well as the information you provide about each party if you do this.

- When introducing people, it's crucial to remember to pronounce their names correctly.

- Offer to shake hands.

- Use titles when necessary. It is preferable to refer to people by their titles in more formal or professional contexts, such as "Mr.," "Mrs.," "Miss," or "Dr." It might be appropriate to omit each person's title in a more relaxed or sociable atmosphere.

## RESTAURANT ETIQUETTE AND TABLE MANNERS

Even though we all like dining out with family and friends, it's crucial to learn the conventions of doing so.

You might find yourself attending a lot of formal dinners since you might attend birthday and graduation parties. So, knowing proper table etiquette is a vital skill for now and in the future when you have to attend business meetings and banquets.

Here are some helpful guidelines to keep in mind when dining out:

- Shake hands or smile at the head waiter as they enter.

- Dress appropriately.

- The napkin must be put on your lap, either before or after placing the order, after you are seated at the table.

- Chew quietly, slowly, and politely without creating any noise.

- Leave the table and use the restroom if you need to groom yourself.

- If you share a plate at a restaurant, be considerate of the person you share your food with.

- Phone use is discouraged unless there is an emergency.

- While talking before the food arrives is acceptable, talking while your mouth is full is not.

- Gum doesn't belong on the edge of your plate, inside your napkin, and most definitely not on (or under) the table; it belongs in the trash.

- Keep critical remarks to yourself.

In the environment we live in today, maintaining manners and etiquette is crucial and helps you develop into a lovely and pleasant adult.

## HOW TO LEAVE A TIP

Is there a standard tipping amount for hairstylists? What about the delivery guy?

Here, we'll go over when it's proper to leave a tip, when it isn't, and how much to leave (Vandal, 2023).

### RECOMMENDED TIPS FOR RESTAURANT

In a restaurant, a tip of 10–15% percent of the tab is customary. No matter how well the service was, it is polite and kind to leave a tip.

Some restaurants and diners won't take separate checks from groups of people dining together. Therefore, you should tip in addition to paying for your meal when paying by cash.

### TAXI AND RIDESHARE TIPS

In cabs, tips are frequently between 15–20% percent of the fare, or $1 or $2. A $2 tip is typical for ridesharing services like Uber and Lyft.

### HOTEL TIPPING PROTOCOLS

Leave $2 or $3 per day rather than a large tip at the end of your stay for housekeeping. It is only reasonable to leave a tip each day, as the cleaner who cleans your room one day might not be the same one who cleans your room the following.

### TIP AMOUNTS AT HAIR AND NAIL SALONS

You may leave 15% (max) of the overall tab in salons. Remember that many places only accept cash tips.

### FOOD DELIVERY

Since most delivery apps already include an in-app tipping feature, it's simple to add the customary 15–20% tip. There is also a difference between a delivery fee and a tip.

### TIPS IN COFFEE SHOPS

Even though rounding up the cost of your hot beverage order is not required, doing so is appreciated, particularly if you are a regular customer or the barista went above and beyond to make your visit memorable.

## ADVICE ON HOW TO LEAVE A TIP ON A LITTLE AMOUNT

So what if you end up paying more than $3 for your breakfast?

Ignore the 20% guideline and leave at least $1 to be safe. Naturally, we might try to minimize costs wherever we can, yet tipping is still considered polite. More people will notice a $1 tip than no tip at all. No matter how large the bill is, a decent tip should always be left when dining out.

## FIVE PEOPLE TO NEVER TIP

Workers should be tipped for good service and effort, but there are some situations in which this is inappropriate. Here are five such people:

- teachers
- medical specialists (nurses, doctors, therapists)
- package-delivery people
- sports coaches and camp counselors
- employees

## WHAT TO DO IF YOU'RE NOT HAPPY WITH THE LEVEL OF SERVICE

Maybe your hairdresser made the coloring in your hair too bright, or your waitress almost sent you on a trip to the hospital if you didn't see the peanut in your muffin that you are highly allergic to, even after telling her. You don't have to hush up about your dissatisfaction, but don't try to talk them out of a tip. Explain your disappointment while keeping in mind that mistakes are human nature. It's fine to leave a 10% smaller tip than normal (but no less).

## WHEN YOU HAVE NO EXTRA CASH, SHOULD YOU LEAVE A TIP?

Should you tip if you don't have any additional cash isn't the question. The real question is: Should we go out to eat right now? Suppose you had $15, but your burger cost $14. The burger is too expensive for you. You may believe you can, but you cannot.

Dinner plus tip equals the price of your meal.

*Segue: In this chapter, we focused on the importance of manners and etiquette and how to practice these skills for a better future. In the next chapter, we'll take an interesting dive into dating.*

# WORDS MATTER

One of the most important ways to be polite to someone is in the way that you speak to them. Aside from the standard "please" and "thank you", what are some additional words and phrases that can help show that you are a kind and polite individual?

# Chapter 4: The Delicate Discussing of Dating and Daughters

> You are very powerful, provided you know how powerful you are.
> —Yogi Bhajan

Do you think you'd like to start dating? Wait, that was a trick question. The real question is: As you were thinking about dating, did someone in particular spring to mind and have you grinning ear to ear or blushing uncontrollably? If yes, then congratulations! You have yourself a crush.

But before you assume that you've found your happily ever after, remember that this is only the simple part. Being in a relationship can be really satisfying, but it also requires a lot of patience and effort.

So, in this chapter, we'll explore all the facets of teen dating, what you should do, and what to run away from.

## How to Confess Your Feelings Without Making Things Weird

It can be thrilling but sometimes daunting to tell someone you like them, and let's be honest, it's not always simple. What if they don't like you back? What if they're not the person you thought they were? What if your best friend likes them too?

There's much to consider when dating, especially knowing that building a relationship is more than just liking someone and takes real dedication, trust, and effort for it to work.

There are a few ways to let your crush know that you're into them, even if it could feel frightening and overwhelming.

These suggestions can help you make this confession as simple as possible.

## GIVE SOME HINTS

If you're nervous about admitting to your crush, drop hints and see how they react. Make eye contact and hold it if you pass them in the corridor. After school, flirtatiously text or tease them to show you're thinking about them. It may ease tension and make your crush want to get closer.

## SET A DEADLINE FOR YOURSELF

Be accountable. Set a deadline to contact your crush. If anxiety gets the better of you, you may put it off too long. If so, pick a date and set a deadline to tell them how you feel.

## PRACTICE SAYING WHAT YOU INTEND TO

Preparation never hurts, right? Though rare, planning your response and even mentally practicing it before speaking may make you feel less apprehensive. If you write, try a diary or your phone.

## GIVE THEM ROOM TO EXPRESS THEIR EMOTIONS

Express your feelings without expecting a response. Don't worry if they don't instantly respond. Your crush may respond immediately or take time to understand their emotions.

## TALK TO YOUR FRIENDS

Your best friend's pep talk can fix everything, especially if you're self-conscious or unsure of how you feel. Before confessing to a crush, talk to your friends. Do you genuinely like this person, or do you just like the idea of being in a relationship?

## TAKE A BROAD PERSPECTIVE

It can be upsetting to think your crush has changed their mind about you. It's okay if you're rejected or ignored. It'll get better, trust me. It may help to remind yourself that it's better to know if your crush doesn't like you than to keep yearning for someone who doesn't. You're valuable regardless of your crush's opinion.

# Cute Ways to Ask Your Crush Out

Having a crush can seem like a magical thing. Almost everything about them will feel and seem perfect, from the way they smiles to the way they walk. Yet, you have no idea how to spend time with them. Maybe what you really want is to hang out, but you have no idea how to approach someone at this point.

Don't worry, though. Here is a collection of unique and interesting ways to ask someone out on a date. While these ideas may sound daunting at first, they are actually rather simple and effective once you get the hang of them (Pai, 2022).

### SEND INNOCENT AND SWEET MESSAGES

If you're too nervous to ask him out in person, try sending them a sweet message instead. You may text something vague like, "I like you," or something more direct like, "I have feelings for you."

You can also try to sneak some cute notes onto their desk or in their locker. Try your best to write something that'll make them smile. They might be blown away by your effort.

### TRY POETRY

Talk about the nineteenth century! Am I right? But in truth, some things just don't fade away, including love poetry. Use poetry to express how you feel. It's fine to sing cheesy love songs to them as long as they come from the heart. Try to prompt them to text or call you if they like your effort. Don't forget to draw a heart at the end!

### GET THEIR HELP

The easiest way to trick a crush into talking to you and going out is to ask for their assistance with something you know they will enjoy doing. After that, take them out for ice cream or invite them over for dinner on your front porch. Still, try not to come out as desperate.

### TELL THEM YOU'RE HUNGRY

It's okay to annoy your friends with your declaration of hunger over and over. So, if your crush happens to be your friend, let it be known that you are indeed hungry. Tell them you don't like eating alone or that you're excited to try a new place, and you'll immediately have a date. Let them know how you feel by talking to them first.

### GIVE THEM AN "EXTRA TICKET"

Find out what kind of sports or entertainment they like, buy a ticket for two, and say that you have a "spare." There, you have a date!

### GET CREATIVE AND USE A PICK-UP LINE

Pick-up lines are cheesy, but many people do have an odd sense of humor. Your crush might like it if you use a pick-up line on them. Make them laugh!

### FIND OUT IF YOU HAVE ANYTHING IN COMMON

Talking to someone with a common interest can be fun. When they're interested in you, they'll take the time to get to know you and focus entirely on you.

### MAKE A JOKE

Maybe your crush is your best friend—it happens. Try to make them laugh while you tell them how you feel. You should take advantage of their sincerity if you can.

### ALLOW A FRIEND TO INTRODUCE YOU

If it is tough to get in touch with your crush, see if you have any mutual friends. They can introduce you two.

### GET A "WING WOMAN"

Maybe you can ask your friend to talk to your crush for you. It's possible that your best friend would feel at ease playing cupid and addressing a potential suitor on your behalf.

### GO ON A DOUBLE DATE

If you're nervous about asking out your crush on a solo date, you could always invite several of your friends along.

## Planning Your First Date

You should enjoy dating. You shouldn't be stressed, hurting, or living like you're married with three kids. Use your youth to build healthy relationships with family, friends, and possible life-long partners. Your experiences will help you find true love and healthy relationships.

So, here is all you need to know to start dating the right way.

## BEFORE YOU START DATING

Before dating, write out what you desire in a good person. Make a detailed list of everything you should and shouldn't have done. Evaluate what you can give a possible new friend as you consider a date.

## THE INITIAL DATE

Once you know your ideal match, plan your first date. Make basic plans before asking someone out. Since dating requires risk and forethought, the more you do in advance, the better. Before your first big date alone, talk to your parents about expectations, and plan where and when.

## LUST VS. LOVE

Teens often confuse love and lust. This substantially complicates teen dating. Love can be empathy, friendship, or family. Teen love requires finding someone who likes and understands you. Lust is a temporary, powerful physical attraction. Hormones and sexual desire inspire teen passion. It's a natural mental aspect of growing up, yet it may also be incredibly strong and perplexing.

Keeping a positive attitude and acknowledging these feelings will help.

## TIPS FOR TEEN DATING

Consider the following simple tips before you go on your first date:

- Every romantic relationship requires communication.
- Don't assume and refrain from rumors.
- Indicate whether your relationships are casual or exclusive.
- Move on if you are declined or rejected; don't waste time dwelling on it.
- Get to know someone a little before approaching them about a date. It will be simpler to determine what they might respond to.

# Fun, Non-Awkward First Date Ideas

What you do on a first date can be incredibly nerve-racking. What if you run out of topics to talk about? What should you wear? However, first dates are enjoyable and can be the sowing ground for something bigger. Choosing the right venue and activity will allow you and your crush to feel comfortable. Even if dinner and a movie are your go-to first date, you want it to be special.

If you need an ideal first date, try these fun, non-awkward first date ideas.

### SKATING RINK

As you enter the ice skating rink, huddle up and grasp one another. This date will undoubtedly help to break the ice (sorry, I had to).

### BOWLING

Go bowling and get competitive to see who can score the most points in ten frames.

### ATTEND AN ART CLASS

Attend an art class to spark your imagination. You can bond while making something artistic and take home a souvenir of the date.

### PLAY SOME GAMES

A game night is the only thing that brings out your real self. Have fun and playfully trash-talk your date a little. It'll make you laugh right away.

### VISIT AN ESCAPE ROOM

You'll be too busy trying to solve puzzles and escape the area before time runs out to have any awkward pauses or breaks in the conversation.

### COOK TOGETHER

Instead of going to a restaurant, make your own dinner together (with permission, of course). You can show off your cooking skills and have fun.

### TAKE A WALK

Walking with your date lets you talk and connect. A lovely neighborhood is also ideal.

## GO ROLLERBLADING

Put on some knee protection and take a spin around the block. You're certain to have a great time and laugh a lot.

## KARAOKE

Sing your favorite songs and show off your skills at karaoke. Have fun choosing a romantic duet.

## VISIT A FARMERS' MARKET

On a nice day, eat fresh foods and attend a farmer's market with your date to get ingredients for a family dinner.

## VISIT A TRAMPOLINE PARK

Jump around and enjoy your date. After reliving your childhood, get some pizza to relax.

## VISIT THE BEACH

Get your swimsuit and head to the beach. Nothing is more flirtatious than a lighthearted water fight.

## GET DESSERT

Enjoy some treats together! Choose your favorite dessert spots in the neighborhood and go.

## SUPPORT A SPORTS TEAM

Grab some inexpensive tickets to a game. You can have some hot dogs while rooting for your team.

## GO ON A HIKE

Take pleasure in the clean air and stunning scenery.

## VOLUNTEER

Do good while getting to know one another.

## CHECK OUT A STREET FAIR

Visit a neighborhood street fair to eat delicious foods. It's the ideal outdoor experience that doesn't cost any money.

## VISIT AMUSEMENT PARKS

There are tons to do at an amusement park. There are rides, activities, and delicious snacks. Without either of you being aware of it, your date will last for several hours.

## VISIT AN ART GALLERY

Visit an art gallery to take in some magnificent artwork with your date.

## GO TO A CONCERT

Listen to some live music and get to know one another. This first date will live in your memory forever.

## VISIT AN ANTIQUE STORE

You'll have a blast and leave with something nice! Make it a contest to see who can find the cutest item under $20.

## OFFER TO WALK DOGS AT SHELTERS

Because many shelters rely on volunteers to exercise their canine inmates, this outdoor activity is excellent for a first date.

## GO TO A CAT CAFE

Enjoy a day with feline friends with your date. You'll love how great your decision was.

## TAKE A COURSE

You can do any class type! The basics of ceramics, acrobatics, or a different language! You'll also have an excuse to hang out every week.

## VISIT THE TOP-RANKED TOURIST ATTRACTION IN YOUR AREA

It'll be a memorable experience while having fun!

# Dating Advice

Love is the strongest emotion. Despite the thrill of love, teenage relationships may be challenging, especially for girls.

Getting into a relationship as a young lady without assistance might leave you heartbroken and full of regrets. The right tools and advice, including dating dos and don'ts, will help you negotiate the difficult dating climate. Please note that dating and falling in love are different, although one might lead to the next. Either way, healthy relationships involve more than the initial sparks and butterflies.

Wouldn't it be nice to know how to avoid the blunders most teen girls make when dating? You can use these dating tips to build a long-lasting, healthy relationship and avoid frequent problems.

## KNOW (AND BE) WHO YOU ARE

Without a moral identity, dating (or any other journey in life, for that matter) is difficult.

Due to social media and culture, many teens succumb to peer pressure and struggle with the need to fit in. You might even complain about your height, legs, and breasts or feel strange about your voice. This won't work in a relationship. Start with honesty, and never pretend. Loving others begins with self-love.

## NEVER ASK FOR LOVE

Never beg for love. Never do this if you value your dignity. Being confident in what you can offer in a relationship isn't arrogance—it's knowing your worth.

Know that you will ultimately have to confront the misery of accepting that someone isn't into you the way you're into them and move on, whether it's a crush who doesn't share your sentiments or a boyfriend who has fallen out of love with you.

## AVOID RUSHING

If you're not ready, don't hurry into dating because relationships have a lot of responsibility. Love is a marathon, not a race. If you can see yourself with the other person for a long time, that's a good sign.

You can only do so much as a teenager before a certain age. When you start a career, travel, and meet gorgeous and God-fearing people, you'll probably start to see life differently (perhaps differently from your partner). So, go slowly.

## CREATE BOUNDARIES

Too many adults and teens fail this. No boundaries breed disrespect. If you reduce your standards to accommodate someone, it's hard to change their behavior.

Maturity is not always age-related. Real maturity requires personal boundaries and beliefs.

Early in the relationship, discuss some issues. What are your must-dos and no-nos? If someone loves you, they should keep their word. Period!

## NEVER LET YOUR STANDARDS SLIP

You show other people how to treat you by the things you tolerate.

Having these boundaries in place is essential for a successful relationship. Even better, sharing these restrictions or criteria with a trusted friend or mentor is a terrific approach to maintaining accountability.

## PAY ATTENTION

When you're together, make sure your partner never feels alone. Presentness is rare today. True love is being there for someone through good and bad. Being there matters, whether you're celebrating or struggling.

## REMEMBER YOUR FRIENDS

After dating, some people ditch all their friends. Nobody wants a friend who would dump her for someone else, so keep your social life apart from your partner.

## DON'T RUN AWAY FROM ISSUES

Don't worry about relationship problems. Problems don't always end relationships. Avoiding problems worsens them. Accepting mistakes, discussing them, and fixing them is better. Do something even if it feels strange. It will get easier because strong relationships require conflict resolution.

## LEARN HOW TO SPOT TOXIC RELATIONSHIPS

If you're in an abusive relationship, your boyfriend might

- berate you and make you feel horrible all the time
- keep you away from your family and friends
- check your messages

- monitor your location and conversations on social media, and make threats that something terrible will happen if you break up
- make you do things you don't want to
- guilt-trip you
- hurt you

### IMPROVE ONE ANOTHER'S QUALITY OF LIFE

Nobody doesn't want to be their best. Relationships are important for progress, but not everyone realizes it. You emulate those you associate with.

Most people attribute their successes and failures to their relationships. Date to improve each other's life.

He's good if he makes you want to be a better girl. However, if your relatives and friends constantly criticize your behavior around your partner, it may be time to reconsider your relationship.

### LOVE ISN'T SEX

This ought to be obvious, but regrettably, it isn't. A lot of adults wish they had realized that "sex isn't love" sooner. Thus, you must define your expectations in advance. Never give in to pressure.

Our culture supports the contrary. They may mock you if you don't have sex like everyone else, but understand that "sleeping with you" does not necessarily mean that the person loves you.

## Safety Tips

For your dating safety, it's best to sit with your parents and set some rules. This allows you to keep safe while your parents let you date.

Below are the most important tips for safety.

### HAVE A CURFEW

Curfews are a simple way to set boundaries and give you a scheduled time to get home. They may suck at first, but they really are important for safety.

## NEGOTIATE GROUND RULES

As you begin dating, it's crucial that you follow some ground rules. Discuss your parent's expectations.

For example, if you're going on a date and you change your mind and go to the movies instead of a party, you should let your parents know.

## LET YOUR PARENTS MEET YOUR DATE

Most teens refuse to introduce their dates to their parents. However, safe dating requires this step. This protects you if you wish to date someone you met on social media.

Invite your date to your house or dinner on a Friday night. These casual interactions let your parents learn more about your dates and see how you interact. Remember to trust their judgment, no matter how much you like a guy.

## LET YOUR PARENTS BE A STANDING EXCUSE FOR YOU

You might find yourself in circumstances where dates don't go as planned. Maybe your date took you to a drug and alcohol party. They might be abusive, rude, or pressuring you for sex. If your parents are your go-to defender, you can "blame" them for leaving or picking you up.

Some parents use a code phrase or text to alert them when their kids need help. If you call or text them this term, they'll call you and justify picking you up.

This built-in escape route will help you avoid peer pressure.

## LET OTHERS KNOW WHERE YOU ARE

Never go on a date without someone, even your best friend, knowing where you're going. Always tell your parents about dating plans.

Phones can be turned off, lose power, or lose service if something should go wrong.

# How To Respectfully Break Up With Someone

The beginning of a relationship is always thrilling. A new relationship's exhilaration might outweigh everything.

However, newness eventually fades. As a relationship grows closer, things change. Some people have happy, committed relationships, while other relationships fail.

Breakups happen to most people. Anyone who has gone through it knows it's painful, even when it's for the best. But it's true that if (or when) that bridge comes, it's rather hard to cross.

So, below, we'll look at a few tips on how to end a relationship.

## BREAK-UP DOS AND DON'TS

Every relationship varies and ends differently. However, there are several "dos and don'ts" to consider when having that break-up chat.

DO:

- Consider your desires and why. Reflect on your feelings and decisions. Even though it hurts others (not just him, but if his family loved you as well), you're choosing what's best for you.

- Consider your next remarks and the other person's response. Will you surprise your boyfriend? Will he be sad, mad, hurt, or happy? Sensitivity means considering the other person's feelings. So, it helps to prepare.

- Let them know you care. Consider conveying sincerity, friendliness, awareness, respect, and caring as you speak.

- Avoid harsh honesty. Tell them what you like about them. Give your reason for breaking up. Honesty isn't cruel. Think about being honest and kind.

- Be present. Breaking up in person shows respect and good character. If you live far away, call or video chat. Facebook and SMS may make breaking up easy, but consider how you'd feel if your boyfriend did that to you.

- If it helps, trust someone. Talking to a trusted friend may help. Make sure your trusted friend can keep it a secret until you break up.

DON'T:

- Don't avoid the other person or the conversation. Dragging things out makes things harder for you and your partner. Knowledge may also spread when people delay. Never let someone else tell your ex about the breakup.

- Don't rush into difficult topics.

- Don't disrespect them. Discuss your ex nicely. Don't slander them. You never know—your ex may become a friend in the future or rekindle your romance.

These rules apply beyond breakups. If someone asks you out, but you're not interested, use the same methods to respectfully decline.

## HOW TO SPEAK AND WHAT TO SAY

You're breaking up. After choosing when to talk, figure out how to do it politely, fairly, honestly, and with care. Breakups require preparation beyond words.

Here are a few phrases you might use. Use these concepts and adapt them to your needs and preferences:

- Tell them that you need to discuss something important.

Start by telling them you appreciate them. For instance, "You're important to me, and we've been close. I'm glad we met."

- Tell him what's broken (your reason for the break-up). "I'm not ready for a serious boyfriend yet," or "I can't accept that you cheated on me."

- Say you want to split up. "I wish to split up," for instance. "I'd like to stay friends but not your girlfriend."

- Apologize if this hurts. For instance, "I wouldn't hurt you. I'm sorry this isn't what you expected" or "I'm sorry if this offends you, and I realize this is hard to hear."

- Use kind words. For instance, "You'll be okay. I'm sure we'll always care about each other." You can also add, "I'll never forget our good times. I'm glad we met."

- Consider their words. Be patient, and don't be surprised if the other person becomes angry or dissatisfied after hearing you.

- Give space. Send your ex a lovely message or start a chat to show you care.

Whether short or long-term, relationships have value. Every relationship teaches us about ourselves and our ideal partner.

Breakups also offer learning opportunities, although they are complex. Ending a relationship enhances our ability to have difficult conversations.

*Segue: In this chapter, we looked at the dynamics of dating, some great first date ideas, and general advice to stay safe during teen dating. In the next chapter, we'll explore the dynamics of job hunting and how to land a job with ease.*

# YOUR IDEAL MATE

Dating is hard - and sometimes we get lost in whether or not a potential mate will like us or not. But what if we don't like them? It's just as important to know what we sort of qualities we are looking for in someone we are dating. Here's a chance to make a list of the qualities we seek. But keep in mind that not every single quality needs to be present. Remember - no one's perfect.

# Chapter 5: How To Land Your First Job Like A Pro

Imagine getting your first job (that you adore). Then, you are paid your first paycheck, and you can now begin buying your own little things. It's such a great feeling of victory, accomplishment, and independence.

Now, you may be wishing you were that lucky. But what if I told you that you could be?

Yes. In this chapter, we'll learn how to apply for, land, and keep your dream job.

## Choosing the Perfect Job for You

One of the greatest things about your first job is that it helps you to determine what career path you'd like to take. You can learn skills, earn money, and figure out your future careers by working.

If you wish to obtain a job, you should first learn how to find one that matches your interests, talents, and preferences. Choosing the perfect job isn't easy, but knowing everything about job-hunting should help.

### TYPES OF JOBS FOR TEENAGERS

Teenagers seeking work may take into account many job categories, including the following (Indeed Editorial Team, 2021):

- **Part-time:** A part-time job is usually working fewer than 40 hours per week. They are best if you're looking for something to do after class or on the weekends.

- **Contract:** Contractual employment lasts for a month or a total of 10 weeks.

- **Seasonal:** Just as the name suggests, these jobs are seasonal. While ski resorts typically hire throughout the winter, camps typically do so during the summer.

- **Internships:** These are temporary employment that supports people while they complete school or training for a particular field. Some internships are paid, while others solely count toward course credit.

- **Entrepreneurship:** Something you might want to do is create a business. You can work as a babysitter, start an online store, make crafts and sell them, or be a dog walker, freelance writer, or photographer.

- **Volunteer:** Building your résumé, professional network, and skill set while looking for work is a terrific idea.

## DETERMINE WHAT TYPE OF JOB YOU WANT

Think about what kind of job you desire before you start applying for them. Consider many different factors. Here are just a few:

- **Job Schedule:** You may keep your income steady all year long by working part-time. An internship or temporary position may be ideal if you're looking to increase your work hours over the summer.

- **Skills:** You should think about the skills you wish to acquire on the job.

- Abilities and interests: Think about the several careers that would be a good fit for your skills and interests. If you enjoy working with animals, being a dog walker or an assistant at a vet's office could be a good fit for you.

- **Workplace:** Your work environment consists of the people you work with and the business you do business with.

## WHERE TO LOOK FOR JOBS

Start your job search once you've determined the kinds of positions you're interested in. There are numerous ways and resources you can use to look for work, including the following (Indeed Editorial Team, 2021):

- **Job boards online:** The use of online job boards has allowed businesses to advertise available positions.

- **Newspapers:** Advertisements for available jobs can be found in print publications like newspapers and magazines.

- **Websites:** The best way to apply for a job is to look at the company's website. Some businesses advertise job opportunities online.

- **Shops:** Job postings may be advertised in store windows or on bulletin boards. Inquire if an entry-level position is available with the store's management or owner.

## START BUILDING YOUR NETWORK

Create a professional network. Your network could consist of everyone from your teachers and coaches to your relatives and next-door neighbors. Get information about available jobs from your contacts. They may also be able to point you in the direction of relevant conventions and workshops.

# How to Apply for a Job

Now that you know what to look for when hunting for the perfect job, how exactly do you apply when you actually find this job?

In this section, you'll learn all you need to know about applying for a perfect job.

## GET A WORK PERMIT

Most times, you need a permit to work. Whether or not you need a permit depends on the type of work you do, where you live, and your age. Ask around and learn if a work permit is required in your country and in your chosen field.

## MAKE A RESUME

There is no way around the requirement of a resume once you've decided to enter the job market. It is a synopsis of your professional strengths, such as your training, education, and experience. If you don't have much professional experience, you can still demonstrate to employers why you're competent through things like awards, accomplishments, interests, languages, and volunteer experience.

## HOW TO CREATE A RESUME

You can use all aspects of your life on your resume, showing that you have the skills a recruiter is searching for. The following are some guidelines to remember as you create your resume:

- **Study the job description:** Use the job description to focus your resume on recruiters' priorities. Use keywords to showcase your most relevant talents and experience.

- **Display your contact info:** Ensure your contact information is clear for recruiters. This includes name, address, phone number, and email. If you don't use your street address, just give your town and state. Your email address should be professional and include your name. Your age, Social Security number, and other irrelevant details don't need to be on your resume. If you get the job, the company will ask for more information.

- Professional summary: If you don't have much experience, include a professional summary. This should be one to two phrases that grab a recruiting manager's attention, introduce you, and demonstrate your suitability for the job. You can customize your professional summary for each position. Start with a powerful adjective like

    - enthusiastic
    - dedicated
    - energetic
    - self-motivated
    - customer-oriented

For instance, "Honor roll student looking for a part-time server job at Flower Diner to show off my customer support and time management skills. A friendly team player who thrives under pressure."

- Add relevant sections: You don't need to use all the sections on your resume unless they're relevant. You can always list talents, and if you have a relevant hobby or interesting experience, you can enhance these parts. Common resume sections include

    - Work history: List your occupations from your most recent ones, with bullet points describing your duties.
    - Education: List your school, diplomas, and related courses.
    - Skill: List your strong areas and talents.
    - Awards and accomplishments: List your accomplishments, such as making the dean's list or winning a school contest.
    - Hobbies and interests: Include them if they pertain to the job.

- Volunteer experience: Teens often lack professional work experience, but you may have relevant experience through helping at school or in your community. Include the organization, role, dates, and a brief summary of your volunteer activities.

- Provide data if possible: Discuss your accomplishments' impact. Mention your high GPA. You can demonstrate great leadership by leading the debate team to a perfect record.

- Proofread your resume: Spellcheck your resume to spot mistakes. Read your resume aloud to catch errors, and if possible, have someone else examine it.

## TIPS FOR WRITING A RESUME FOR TEENAGERS

Your CV should convey your work ethic to the employer. You don't want people to waste time understanding what you've written. So, here's what you need to do:

- **Use simple formats and fonts:** For help, use a resume template. They might help you decide what to include and how to format your resume. The recruiting manager will prefer your information in Times New Roman, Arial, or Calibri.

- **Consider employer needs:** If you're looking for a camp counselor position, stress your child-care experience. Emphasize customer service and teamwork in your waiter application.

- **Use powerful verbs:** Action words describe your accomplishments. Instead of detailing your accomplishments, words like led, studied, tutored, and created emphasize your significance.

- **Use one page:** Keep it brief so employers can understand.

- **Save as a PDF:** Save as a PDF for platform-independent formatting.

## ADD A COVER LETTER

Job applications require a one-page cover letter. Unless the job advertisement indicates otherwise, always include a cover letter.

It's basically a brief letter expressing your interest in the job and showing your qualifications. Your cover letter and resume are your first impressions to companies, so it should be clear, concise, and well-written. While not all jobs require cover letters, writing one might help you stand out.

## COVER LETTERS' PURPOSE

Cover letters should

- introduce yourself and state the position you're seeking
- show that your talents and experience match the job requirements
- encourage the reader to review your resume
- end with a call to action (for example, asking for an interview or a meeting)

## COVER LETTER CONTENT

Here are a few things that should be included in your cover letter:

- **Name and contact:** Start your cover letter with your contact information. Email and phone number are required, but your postal address is not.

- **Recruiter's name and contact:** Include the person's name, job, and firm name under your own name and contact information. Call the company if you can't find this information. Use "To whom it may concern" solely as a last option.

- **Job title:** Start your cover letter with the job you want. For example, "Regarding application for Customer Care Rep."

- **Your relevant talents:** Briefly describe how your qualifications match the job description. A brief bullet list works.

- **Your qualifications for the position:** After describing your talents and experience, explain why you're suitable for the job (e.g., "My ability to interact with everyone and my experience in managing customer problems in a retail context make me well qualified for this job").

- **Use their language:** Using a job's language demonstrates that you understand the employer's industry.

- **Request a call:** Asking the recruiter to read your resume should conclude your cover letter. Then, request an interview. Try, "I have included my resume for your review. I'm eager to hear about this employment."

## COVER LETTER WRITING TIPS

Here are a few more tips to help perfect your cover letter:

- **Determine the recipient:** Avoid writing "To whom it may concern." Find out who will review your application. Though difficult, it's worth it.

- **Learn more about the role:** Contact the recruiter and ask questions. This will help you tailor your cover letter and resume. Is the job team-based? Who would supervise you if hired?

- **Learn about the company:** To customize your cover letter, research the firm. Search the company's name online and visit the corporate website, especially the "About Us" page.

- **Overusing "I":** Use "I believe," "I have," and "I am" sparingly. It's about helping the employer, not you. Read your letter and remove or rework as many "I" lines as possible.

- **Don't discuss other job applications:** Avoid discussing other job applications. Your letter should show the employer you want the job.

## SUBMIT APPLICATIONS

Job applications are accepted both online and in person. Send out two to three applications every day or ten to fifteen each week. With an increase in applications comes the possibility of a rise in employer interest.

Make sure your application is set apart from the rest by submitting a resume and cover letter that stands out. Passion for the work will shine through for potential employers. Read the posting carefully to learn what the employer is looking for, and then be sure to highlight the areas of your application where you excel.

Want the perfect application? Try these on for size.

### THERE'S NO RUSH

Wait. Before filling out your application, list all the required details. Fill it out slowly to avoid missing anything.

### SHOW THE EMPLOYER YOU CAN FOLLOW DIRECTIONS

Complete all application areas. N/A or "not applicable" can be used for boxes without information. Make sure you understand the questions.

### EMPHASIZE TIMELINESS AND ATTENDANCE

If possible, mention flawless attendance and timeliness.

### GET REFERRALS

Prepare these names! Most employers require 3–4 references that can attest to your work ethic and responsibility. Ask babysitters, teachers, or coaches if you have never worked. If you want to use someone as a reference, let them know.

### CHECK FOR FOLLOW-UPS ON YOUR PHONE

Make sure your voicemail greeting is appropriate for an employer before providing your phone number on the application. Check your messages often to avoid missing a call for an interview!

### PREPARE FOR INTERVIEWS OR JOB TESTS

If you've never been interviewed, it can be hard to prepare, but practicing will help you get hired.

Reviewing common interview questions might help teens prepare for employment interviews. Reviewing replies helps you formulate your own. Personalize your answers to reflect you as a person and a job seeker.

### TYPICAL TEEN INTERVIEW QUERIES

Here are 10 of the most popular teen job interview questions and good replies. Please note that you don't have to (and shouldn't) study the response word-for-word. They are simply there to help you know how to answer a question (Doyle, 2022).

### 1. Why Are You Job-Hunting?

Making money is a motivating factor for everyone, but your motivations for applying should demonstrate your interest in the field or desire to grow professionally.

**Your response:** "Drawing is my favorite hobby. I want experience at the art gallery to decide if I can go to art school and become an artist."

### 2. Why Are You Applying to Our Company?

Companies often use this question to gauge a candidate's dedication to and familiarity with a particular field. In any case, familiarizing yourself with the company's work, culture, and ideals through its website is a good first step.

**Your response:** "I want to become an engineer; thus, I'd like to work at a top electricity company to learn how to work with skilled workers in the area."

### 3. How Has Your Education Prepared You to Work for Our Business?

Companies often use this question to gauge a candidate's dedication to and familiarity with a particular field.

**Your response:** "I want to work in journaling because English was my favorite high school subject. I was also the editor of my school's paper."

### 4. Why Hire You?

Employers want to ensure they are investing in the right person by investing time in training. Share your interest in working for the firm after graduation and whether or not you see yourself as a good fit for the team.

**Your response:** "Teachers say I work hard. As an honors student, I never miss class and study hard. I'm fast, smart, and adaptable."

### 5. What Qualities Do You Believe Are Necessary for Success in This Position?

Describe your ideal skills and experiences to the interviewer. If your qualifications match those of the open position, you should have no trouble getting hired.

**Your response:** "I became class monitor for three years straight because I'm extroverted and enjoy socializing. I've worked on teams, built morale, and created good experiences through volunteer fundraising and event organizing for our class."

### 6. Do You Have Good Teamwork Skills?

The interviewer will like to hear a teamwork success story.

**Your response:** "I was chosen as team leader in my volunteer group because I love organizing practices and motivating our team."

### 7. What's Your Proudest Achievement?

Don't brag, but discuss an accomplishment that corresponds to the job's qualifications.

**Your response:** "My biggest triumph was getting into university with a full scholarship due to my strong grades and enthusiastic leadership and engagement in high school clubs."

## 8. What Are Your Wage Expectations?

The potential employer is curious as to whether or not your expectations are reasonable. Young workers are likely to receive starting salaries. Don't mention a salary unless you're familiar with that aspect of the position.

**Your response:** "Since my main goal is work experience and perhaps great referrals from you, I'm willing to negotiate my wage. How much did your last entry-level worker make?"

## 9. Tell Me About a Serious Issue You Resolved.

The interviewer wants to know your problem-solving skills.

**Your response:** "Our school's track team made it to nationals one year. But the school couldn't afford a bus, our hotel, or food. So, I contacted everyone's parents and grandparents to explain our transportation crisis. By day's end, I had enough volunteer drivers."

## 10. Have You Struggled With a Boss or Teacher?

The interviewer wants to know how you handle authority. Answer honestly, but give a happy conclusion.

Your response: "I enjoy orchestra and cheerleading. Since practices often conflicted, my captain and band director said I had to choose. I managed to convince them to compromise with me. The band director allowed me to perform in my cheerleading outfit, and my captain let me leave practice early on Tuesdays and Thursdays to attend practice."

### WHAT TO BRING TO AN INTERVIEW

When going to the interview, bring

- a completed application
- working documents
- 2-4 references
- your resume

- a pen and notepad

## JOB INTERVIEW TIPS

Always remember these points when going to a job interview, whether it is your first or twentieth (Doyle, 2022):

- **Be polite:** Keep the interview cheerful and professional by not using foul language, sitting up straight when seated, and shaking hands in the manner we covered earlier.

- **Know your schedule:** The firm will probably want to know what times and days you're available to work.

- **Be timely:** Get to the interview early. Find your destination in advance by obtaining directions. Choose a reliable ride service if you don't have access to a vehicle.

- **Go alone:** Your parents have no business being at a job interview. No one else may assist you as you talk with the interviewer.

## HOW TO IMPRESS

Teens should act like professionals when interviewing. That's the finest method to impress a potential employer and boost your work prospects.

Dress well, answer questions intelligently, and ask questions to make a good impression.

Also, remember to thank your interviewer and send follow-ups after job applications and interviews. A follow-up might show your professionalism and enthusiasm for the job. Wait two weeks before politely contacting a company about a job application.

# General Tips for Applying for Jobs as a Teenager

To close this chapter, here are a few general tips to put you on top of job-hunting, whether it be now or later.

## BE PATIENT

Applying requires patience. It's okay if some employers don't respond or if you're rejected. It's normal. Consider revising your application materials for future jobs or requesting contact for help.

## PRE-APPLY

Apply for employment several months in advance. Job hunting can take weeks or months. It's also vital to know that firms post seasonal jobs months in advance to ensure a full crew throughout their busy season. Apply for summer jobs in early spring.

## BE KIND AND CONFIDENT

Be polite and confident when emailing or meeting potential employers. Though uneasy, expressing confidence can help make a positive first impression. Thanking employers for their time shows courtesy.

## USE CAUTION

As an adolescent, it might be hard to tell a real employment offer from a scam. Protect yourself while job hunting by

- Notifying a trusted friend or parent.
- Pre-visiting the location. Check the event address on a map or visit the *meet-up or interview venue a day before to make sure it's open.*

*Segue: This chapter was quite interesting, as we learned all about job hunting, resume and cover letters, interviews, and nailing your job applications. In the following chapter, we'll take a look at managing your finances in the right and feasible way.*

# BE PREPARED!

We've gone over some interview questions that you may enconter, and some possible answers. Here they are again, but with an opportunity to fill them out yourself, as you would if it were your own interview. This will allow you to work in your own life experiences and personality.

Why are you job-hunting?

_____
_____
_____

Why are you applying to our company?

_____
_____
_____

How has your education prepared you to work for our business?

_____
_____
_____

Why should we hire you?

_____
_____
_____

What qualities do you believe are necessary for success in this position?

_____
_____
_____

Do you have good teamwork skills?

___

What is your proudest achievement?

___

What are your wage expectations?

___

Tell me about a serious issue you resolved.

___

Have you struggled with a boss or teacher?

___

# Chapter 6: Managing Your Money Matters

> IT'S NOT HOW MUCH MONEY YOU MAKE, BUT HOW MUCH MONEY YOU KEEP, HOW HARD IT WORKS FOR YOU, AND HOW MANY GENERATIONS YOU KEEP IT FOR.
>
> —Robert Kiyosaki

---

If you haven't gotten there yet, there will be a time when your parents decide that you're old enough to manage your own money, and whatever change you make at your job will have to finance everything you need.

It'll be okay. They're simply just preparing you for real-life, where managing money is literally your livelihood. That doesn't mean it's easy, though.

Therefore, in this chapter, you'll learn how to budget the right way, save, and manage money properly.

## Budgeting 101

Once you've reached the stage of adolescence, you should budget and develop credit like adults. Teens learning to manage money often make mistakes. And that's okay. It takes advice from parents, knowledge, and experience to learn good financial habits. However, that doesn't mean you shouldn't take the initiative to learn the basics of budgeting.

A budget, as some might know, is a monthly spending plan. Creating a budget might help you avoid debt and overspending. Income and expenses are the foundation of a budget. It helps you to track your income, expenses, and leftovers, which, over time, shows you your spending pattern.

## HOW TO CREATE A BUDGET

Naturally, teen budgets differ from adult budgets. You aren't necessarily earning a wage or budgeting for a mortgage or school loans. However, you can still benefit from knowing how to split your chore or part-time work earnings to cover your costs (Budgeting for teens, n.d.).

### STEP 1: CALCULATE YOUR INCOME

What makes up a budget is the amount of money coming in minus what is spent. The sum of money coming in and going out each month might not be fixed. As such, keeping track of how many things you purchase is essential.

### STEP 2: RECORD YOUR EXPENSES

Knowing your spending habits is the first step in creating a budget. You probably have a good idea of how much money comes in, but keeping track of exactly where it goes could be tricky. Begin with the facts. For at least a week, and preferably a month, save every bill and receipt you get. Use a bullet journal to keep tabs on your spending. Verify purchases and cash withdrawals if you have a bank account.

### STEP 3: DETERMINE YOUR SPENDING PATTERNS

You can determine where you can make cuts in spending without sacrificing necessities. Needs include food, clothing, shelter, transportation, communication, and technology. Spending money on things like takeout, movies, concerts, and video games is wasteful.

### STEP 4: SUBTRACT YOUR SPENDING FROM YOUR EARNINGS

Math time! Yay! To do this, first, determine how much money you're making each week or each month, and then deduct all of your expenses. You'll have a clearer picture of your savings and leisure.

If you've run out of money or are spending more than you earn (gasp!), it's time to revisit your budget and think of ways to cut costs, such as eating in rather than dining out.

### STEP 5: SET SAVINGS GOALS

In other words, you should prepare for the unexpected. It's never too early to start saving for the future. Planning for unexpected costs and savings should be a priority.

## STEP 6: CHOOSE HOW MUCH TO SAVE EACH BUDGET CYCLE

Many strategies exist to determine how much to save.

The 50/30/20 rule is a popular one. You save 20%, spend 50% on needs, and 30% on non-essentials. That's a great feature of budgeting since, at this age, you may not need to spend half your salary on bills! The key is to save at least 20% of your salary.

Reverse budgeting—paying oneself first—is another way. This strategy involves saving a predetermined amount immediately after getting paid.

## STEP 7: STICK TO YOUR BUDGET!

Budgeting becomes less of a struggle as time passes. It's tempting to indulge for more than a week and then "catch up" the following week, but it's not easy to do either. You'll have an easier time and be able to acquire the things you're saving for sooner if you keep to your spending and savings objectives.

## STEP 8: REASSESS AND CHECK IN

Spend some time assessing your finances and progress after a month or two has passed. Assess if your plan is working. If you set a realistic budget, you'll be more likely to stick to it.

## BUDGETING TIPS

Here are some basic tips about budgeting before going further:

- Set achievable money goals. Saving for an iPod can take 3–6 months, while saving for college is a long-term goal.

- Put a photo of your goal on your locker, mirror, or computer desktop. It helps you in temptation!

- Track your spending in a notepad or app (there are many available!).

- Spend according to your income. Borrowing from family doesn't help you create healthy habits while you can!

- If you can't say no to spending money with friends, don't bring extra money and leave your card at home.

# How to Build a Savings Account

Saving early is important. Your current education will equip you to be a financially responsible adult in the future. You should learn about saving and money. Here are a few saving options you have as a teen.

## JOINT ACCOUNTS

Teens often have trouble opening savings accounts or bank accounts.

Savings accounts may seem simple. But bank or credit union accounts require a contract. Minors (under 18 or 21, depending on the state) cannot sign contracts or create bank accounts.

Of course, this does not imply that it is not conceivable. Many individuals under the age of 18 actually have savings accounts. Thus, minors can only open a joint savings account with a parent, grandparent, or guardian. Both of your names stay on a combined account.

After you turn 18, the parent can be removed from the account.

## TEEN SAVINGS ACCOUNT

There are many options for teen checking and savings accounts. You can open a simple savings account with no special qualifications. There is also the option of using a bank account specifically designed for minors.

These savings accounts are called (Higuera, 2022):

- teen savings
- youth savings
- student savings

Despite the name, these accounts let kids start saving early. Teen checking accounts are also available.

## UNIFORM TRANSFER TO MINOR ACT

Teens can save in a custodial Uniform Transfer to Minor Act (UTMA) account. It's not to be confused with a combined checking or savings account. The teen and the adult can share banking responsibilities by opening a joint account. Yet, this account prevents minors from accessing their funds until they reach adulthood.

## OPTIONS FOR WITHDRAWING MONEY FROM YOUR SAVINGS

One can withdraw funds from a bank in a number of different methods, including the following:

### BANK CARD

A debit card is included in the savings account package. This means that deposits and withdrawals are possible.

### MOBILE/ONLINE BANKING

After opening an account, sign up for online banking. Ask your bank if this service is available. Access your account information, including deposits and withdrawals, from any computer or mobile device.

### AUTOMATED SAVINGS FOR TEENS

After deciding on a target savings rate, you have the option of setting up an automatic savings plan. Set aside ten percent of your pay every week, and your money will grow quickly. For example, if your weekly salary is $100, then $10 of that is automatically transferred into your savings account.

## Advice to Start Creating Better Money Habits

As you get older, you realize that though your parents may provide you with money for your ambitions, you may feel better if you can earn and save. This is why financial recommendations for teens are crucial.

### USE TIME WELL

It doesn't matter if you don't have all the money in the world. Time is what is important, and since you are young, your money will have plenty of it. If you have a summer job and save $1,000, you can start a savings account or open it with your parents for a greater interest rate.

### THE CONCEPT OF TIME VALUE OF MONEY

Due to its earning potential, the money you have now is worth more than it will be later. This can help you make smart financial decisions and maximize your money. Financial literacy requires understanding the time worth of money.

You can use this method to manage your savings, assets, and purchasing power.

## GET INTO THE SAVING HABIT

You might be ahead of the rest if your parents saved for your birthdays or college since birth. However, you should keep the trend going. You may walk dogs, babysit, get a job at a diner, or mow lawns in your area as you get older. Get your own source of income and save as you go.

## SAVING TIPS

Manage your finances in numerous ways. We might have the habit of spending small, like a dollar or two, but small purchases add up over time, whether you're spending or saving. In order to save better, follow these tips:

- **Formulate a formula:** Income minus expenses equals savings. You must select whether to minimize expenses or increase revenue to have more money at the end of the month.

- **Reduce your deliveries:** Online food purchasing is popular. However, if you're not attentive, these minor charges might add up.

- **Conserve:** Make monthly deposits into a savings account. You can also automate a check-to-savings transfer when you get paid.

Furthermore, avoid situations that make it hard to say no if you tend to spend without thinking. Plan to have friends over instead of going to the mall, stay away from stores if you're in a foul mood and can't make decent decisions, or don't buy "things" to fit in with specific peers.

## AVOID UNNECESSARY SPENDING

Life involves spending. If you're not careful, you can overspend or get into debt. There are a few important techniques to guarantee that your spending stays in check:

- **Know your costs and list your expenses:** Ask yourself, "What can't I live without?" then prioritize your needs.

- **Follow your values:** Consider your life's value and whether it's worth the expense. If you only eat organic foods and prioritize your health, the extra cost may be worth it.

- **Find options:** You may consider your necessities, then consider how else you can meet them in a less expensive way. To lose weight without a gym membership, for example, you can run or exercise at home.

- **Compromise:** You can reduce your spending on wants, but not altogether. Instead of every weekend, you may enjoy a great dinner with friends once a month.

## HEALTHY MONEY RELATIONSHIPS

You can improve your money relationship in numerous ways. Try these methods.

- **Discuss family finances:** Financial discussions can make people uncomfortable. But avoiding financial troubles is ineffective and might lead to further problems.

- **Practice openness:** Don't hide financial mistakes. Admit to spending all your allowance on unnecessary items. This encourages self-accountability and may lead to financial advice from others.

- **Spend without guilt:** Even when you're budgeting, don't feel guilty about buying necessities (or wants). Sometimes you need to treat yourself and spend outside your budget… just not too much.

- **Avoid financial comparisons with friends:** Comparing your spending and purchases with someone else may lead to wrong assumptions and emotional financial responses. Everyone's spending patterns and financial situations vary.

## CONSIDER COLLEGE

With student loan debt rising, you may choose to delay college or attend community college, which costs less. However, plan from now on and open a college savings account if you plan to attend college. Also, apply for scholarships and paid internships.

## TAKE ADVANTAGE OF YOUR STUDENT ID

Did you know your student ID can get you 10% off at many retailers, such as Apple and Levis? Discounts might save you a lot. If a firm doesn't provide student discounts, ask!

## TAXATION

You can get summer or part-time jobs. Earning your own money boosts your savings and instills responsibility. However, you don't keep all your earnings. You'll have due taxes if you work. Your company deducts this from your compensation, which lowers your take-home pay.

## TAX TIPS

Taxation might be intimidating. After learning the essentials, you'll know what to expect for your salary. You should know net versus gross income. Gross income is your salary pre-tax. These taxes reduce your net income, which is your take-home pay.

Check your tax exemption status. Some income is tax-free.

## PREVENTING DEBT

When it relates to your finances, there's a thin line between being in the white and slipping into the black. While you won't always avoid debt, you can manage it.

Good debt is worth the interest. For example, student loans can help you find a better career and earn more.

Here's how you can prevent debt:

- **Use debit instead of credit:** Borrowing against a line of credit makes it a loan. Late payments attract interest and late fees. However, debit cards allow instant withdrawal from bank accounts.

- **Use credit cards responsibly:** Credit cards help you build credit and get rewards. Use the card to buy things you can pay for in 30 days. Never max out your card, and always pay your bills on time.

- **Credit score matters:** Credit scores show financial management. It evaluates your payment history, punctuality, and debt. Car and home insurance applications may depend on your credit score.

## TEEN FINANCIAL PLANNING

You'll learn to deal with money over time. However, you don't have to learn it all on your own. It's okay to use help.

The Jumpstart Coalition for Financial Literacy offers free financial literacy books, games, teaching plans, and other resources to help you plan, invest and budget your money.

Additionally, Moneytopia is a fun, free online game that teaches teens about money management. A collection of brief video lessons teaches teens about compound interest and apartment costs.

FamZoo is also an award-winning family banking app. It helps teens learn how to earn, save, spend, and donate money in a safe, pleasant atmosphere.

## AVOID IDENTITY THEFT

No one wants to bear the cost of others who practically stole their cards and identity. So, avoid identity theft with these simple actions. This is not only for now but for the future as well. These can be readily incorporated into your routine to protect you and your finances:

- **Review your statements:** To ensure accuracy, check your credit card statements monthly. If your issuer doesn't stop or investigate tiny, sporadic fraud, it might escalate.

- **Avoid disclosing personal details:** Keep personal documents in a secure, private location. To prevent data collection, cut or shred personal documents before throwing them away.

- **Avoid malware:** Install antivirus software to constantly scan for viruses and alien software. Keep software updated.

- **Password-protect:** Most apps and platforms need passwords or PINs. Create sturdy, hack-resistant ones. Avoid using the same password on different platforms or devices. A simple hack might affect all your accounts.

*Segue: This chapter was quite interesting, as we learned how to manage money, budget, save and protect ourselves from financial issues. In the penultimate chapter, we'll learn more about domestic tasks like laundry, cooking, cleaning, and sewing.*

# TIME TO BUDGET

It's time to put what you've learned to the test. Using this worksheet, create your own budget based on possible future income and expenses. This will help you prepare for a future career, lifestyle, and even where you plan to settle down.

Rent _____

Groceries _____

Natural Gas _____

Electricity _____

Water & Sewer _____

Gas _____

Phone _____

Car Insurance _____

Medical Insurance _____

Entertainment _____

Clothing _____

# Chapter 7: Surviving Being Home Alone

- ♥ — ▲ — ♥ — ▲ — ♥ -

Living alone is the ultimate sign of independence. Having the house to yourself might be really fun, which it undoubtedly is, but it also requires a lot of effort. There are a lot of responsibilities, chores, and skills in maintaining a spick-and-span home and living on your own.

So, in this chapter, we'll examine some crucial skills to master before your parents ultimately decide to let you live alone at home for the weekend.

## How to Do Laundry

Doing laundry is a breeze. Modern clothes, detergents, and washing machines make laundry days far less difficult. It's not too soon for you to start learning how to do your own laundry.

### STEPS TO DOING LAUNDRY PROPERLY

The first step is to evaluate whether or not every item of clothing needs to be washed. Maintaining a regular laundry routine is essential, but there are some clothes that can be worn more than once before being washed (Leverette, 2022-a).

### CHECK LABELS

Always read the care labels on your clothing, indicating whether or not an item may be washed in a washing machine.

To dry clean, separate items that say "dry clean only" from those that say "wash separately" or "hand wash." Simply put, it's as easy as that.

### SORT BY COLOR

All the whites, hues, and light grays should go into one pile. Black, scarlet, navy, brown, and dark gray clothes can be sorted separately.

Scrub the stained items in a separate bucket.

## SORT AGAIN

Sort each pile by fabric type. In the white pile, remove towels and linens from clothing. T-shirts, pants, and blouses should be kept separate in dark shades. You can use varied water temps and simplify drying processes by washing by cloth type. Never wash lint-producing and lint-attracting clothes together. It'll just cause more lint!

If you're in a rush and don't have enough goods for a complete washer load of each fabric, wash all articles of each shade together and pick the washer cycle for the most delicate clothes.

## CHOOSE A CLEANER

Choose a cleaner that can be used in a variety of situations. Learn from the directions how much to use based on the weight of your load. Some stains can be pretreated before you wash them. Cleansing agents and washing detergents can help you accomplish this.

## CHOOSE WATER TEMPERATURE AND CYCLE

Unless your garments are particularly dirty, washing them in cold water should get rid of most stains and odors. Hot water is required to remove body oil from only cotton underwear and bed sheets. Do a hot load of laundry once a week to keep your linens and towels clean. Always use cold water to rinse.

Select a wash cycle that is best suited for the fabrics in your laundry basket. While "regular" is appropriate for the vast majority of loads, "permanent press" and "delicate" settings may be required for some fabrics. The term "heavy-duty" is appropriate for use on garments like jeans and bath towels.

## FINAL CHECK

Make sure you have everything you need before starting the laundry. Scan for spills and pre-treat any that you detect. Spot treatments are effective for many stains, while more intensive procedures are necessary for others.

Make sure you have plenty of toilet paper and tissues on hand to prevent any mishaps. To prevent snagging, remove belts and jewelry, take out coins, and fasten buttons and zippers.

## LOADING THE WASHER

Before throwing items into the washing machine, sort them out. If you want clean clothes, don't cram too many items into the washing machine.

## UNLOAD WASHER

In order to prevent wrinkles and mildew, clean laundry should be removed from the washer as soon as possible. When it comes to drying, you have a lot of choices. Clothes can be dried in a dryer, hung up to dry, or flattened out to dry.

## DRYER LOAD

Divide loads by fabric type before drying if you didn't before washing. Choose the right dryer cycle for lightweight and heavy fabric items and dry them together. This prevents shrinking and protects garments.

There are several reasons to line-dry your laundry. Energy savings and clothing protection are the most important. Due to space and weather constraints, not everyone can accomplish this.

## STORE OR HANG

As soon as your clothes are dry, you should either hang them up or put them away. Wrinkles can be avoided by hanging or folding garments immediately after removal from the dryer. Flatten the wrinkles out of your clothes if you need to.

## COMMON LAUNDRY PROBLEMS AND HOW TO FIX THEM

We all make mistakes, but here's help to save the day… or your favorite shirt.

## HOW TO SAVE A SHRUNKEN SWEATER

Most people have accidentally washed or dried a wool or acrylic sweater in hot water and found it shrunk to doll size. This unshrinking method may rescue your sweater before you throw it away or use it for dog clothes.

Fixing a shrunken sweater right after washing is preferable. However, simply air-dry if you can't right away.

Here's what you'll need:

- large tub or sink
- towels
- knitting blocking boards or cork boards

- stainless T-shaped pins
- water
- shampoo or fabric softener

Here's what you do (Leverette, 2022-b):

1. **Ditch the dryer:** Never machine-dry the sweater. Hot dryers permanently shrink sweaters.

2. **Mix a soaking solution:** In a big sink or tub of cool water, combine four tablespoons of baby shampoo or liquid fabric softener.

3. **Submerge the sweater:** Swish it about in the water until it's completely soaked. Set in warm water for 30 minutes to 2 hours.

4. **Don't rinse the sweater:** Squeeze extra moisture without wringing or twisting after removing it from the solution. Drain the sweater solution.

5. **Block sweater:** Put the sweater on a blocking board and use push pins made of stainless steel (to prevent rusting) to gently stretch it back to its original form and size(s). You should pin the sweater every two inches as you move around the outside. Several reshapings may be required.

6. **Dry:** The board should be kept heated but not in direct sunlight. Hang to dry, then reshape as necessary. Perhaps in two days, the sweater will be dry.

7. **Repeat:** If you want to see even more unshrinking, you'll have to start afresh (from the top).

## HOW TO REMOVE DYE STAINS FROM CLOTHES

Oxygen bleach can quickly remove dye stains from clothing that bled on a load of laundry. Oxygen bleach works on washable white and colorful fabrics but not silk, leather, or wool.

Above all, distinguish oxygen bleach from chlorine bleach. Chlorine bleach destroys colors and textiles. However, both liquid and powdered oxygen bleach work nicely.

An old stain can be tougher to remove. So, be sure to get rid of stains as soon as they come.

Here's what you'll need:

- washer
- bathtub or sink
- oxygen bleach (preferably powdered)
- laundry soap

What you'll need to do if they are stained in the washer (Leverette, 2022-c):

1. **Check all loads for stainers:** Remove whatever is making the washer bleed. Don't wash it till you have the right colors.

2. **Rewash affected clothes:** Clothes that have lost their color can be washed in oxygen bleach, such as OxiClean, Nellie's Oxygen Brightener, or Oxo Brite.

3. **Recheck the clothes:** Inspect each item again for traces of dye after washing. Soak and rewash items that have become a different shade.

For dye-stained clothing (Leverette, 2022-c):

1. **Soak stains:** Oxygen bleach and cold water should be combined in a small container based on the manufacturer's recommendations. Let dirty items soak for at least eight hours.

1. **Check and re-soak if needed:** Wash normally if there are no remaining stains. For stains that don't go away after eight hours of soaking in a solution of oxygen bleach and water, wash or soak again. The most efficient method for removing color from fabric without damaging it is to repeat the process several times.

## How to Iron Stuff

Straight, smooth, and immaculate clothing makes a good first impression. Even if it doesn't need to be ironed, clothes look better when ironed.

Make sure your iron is set at the correct temperature by checking the garment's care label before you begin.

Here are some simple steps to iron shirts, slacks, dresses, and skirts.

### IRONING A T-SHIRT

Here's how to iron your favorite t-shirt:

1. Flatten the shirt's collar, chest, and sleeves on the ironing board and press out any wrinkles. Follow this by turning the collar inside out and ironing it.

2. Remove creases from the sleeves by ironing from the underarm seam to the top.

3. Have the iron ready and lay the lower front part of the shirt on the board. The shoulder and armhole seams should be ironed along with the rest of the front. The side seam, back body, opposite side seam, and front all need to be pressed; thus, you should turn the shirt inside out.

## IRONING PANTS

Pressing slacks and pants, creased or not, adds style. Follow these steps for your desired look (Wilson, 2022):

1. Turn your pants inside out and iron the pockets. Pull the trouser top over the narrow end of the ironing board to flatten side seam pockets.

2. Turn the trousers right side out and carefully iron the waist and top by draping the top of the slacks over the narrow end of the board. Iron pockets lightly to hide pocket lines.

3. Stack the pants legs on the ironing board and align seams. Iron the lower leg, then flip and iron again.

4. Align the inseam and outer seam and put the pants on the board for a center crease. Set the crease on each leg's front with steam.

## IRONING SKIRTS AND DRESSES

Pleats, ruffles, and gathers make pressing skirts harder than expected. Dresses may have shirt collars, cuffs, skirt frills, and gathers. These steps allow tasteful ironing of both (Wilson, 2022):

1. Iron the collar, yoke, cuffs, sleeves, and collar top for dresses with sleeves and collars.

2. Start the skirt from the bottom and move up to the waist.

3. Iron the inside of gathered and ruffled skirts from the hemline to the center. Start at the bottom of the inside pleat and go to the outside. Steam sets pleats.

4. Iron around or cover delicate buttons with a spoon. Lay the garment em-

broidered side down on a terry cloth towel or pressing cloth and steam from the other side.

### IRONING TIPS

Here are some simple tips for ironing:

- Set your iron to the shirt's care label's recommended temperature.
- Start with the softest, lowest-temperature materials and work up to the toughest, highest-temperature fabrics. This prevents scorching sensitive textiles with a hot iron because irons take longer to cool down than heat up.
- For smoother results, lightly dampen the fabric before ironing.
- When using spray starch, stay 6–10 inches away from the garment and let it soak in for a minute before pressing for the smoothest results.
- Check the manufacturer's guidelines for water type to avoid buildup, blocked holes, and spitting in your steam iron. Empty the iron before storage.
- After ironing, hang or fold the clothing to avoid wrinkles.

### REMOVING LIGHT SCORCH MARKS ON WHITE CLOTHES

If the scorch mark is caught in its early stages, turn off the iron and use your fingers or a soft bristles brush to apply a heavy-duty laundry detergent, such as Tide or Persil. Wash the garments in the hottest water that is safe for the fabric after 10 minutes (Leverette, 2022).

If the mistake was made later and the scorch stain is minor, you can remove it by wiping it with a clean white cloth dipped in distilled white vinegar. The fabric must be transferred to a clean area while the charred fibers are being removed. Use a white towel dampened with cool water to clean satin.

## How to Sew a Button

When you buy clothes, many include additional buttons in case one falls off. If the thread is hanging on snaps, you can mend it using thread and a needle. Hopefully, it doesn't happen because it's annoying. But just in case, simply get a tiny sewing kit.

## HAND SEWING: THREAD AND TIE

Hand sewing completes many sewing projects. Not all sewing machines can hem or put on a button. So, the first thing we need to do is thread the needle.

### THREADING A NEEDLE

- Insert the needle threader loop into the needle eye.
- Holding the needle and threader in one palm, push the thread through the needle threader until it's four or five inches through.
- Gently draw the needle threader back through the needle eye.

### KNOTTING THE THREAD

Knotting is easy, but you may need to practice:

- Hold the thread between your thumb and index finger.
- Completely wrap the tip of your index finger with a loop of thread and pull through.

### SEWING A BUTTON

Now, sewing the button can seem tricky at first, but it's quite easy!

Use these steps:

- **Thread and knot the needle:** Follow the steps above to complete this step. To hide your work, use a color that matches your shirt, jeans, or skirt. Line up your button. The ridge should be up and the flat part against the fabric.
- **Position your button and insert your needle:** Start by poking up through the fabric and into a buttonhole. Pull the thread through once to anchor the knot.
- **Insert the needle into the opposite buttonhole:** You thread up through the fabric of the first hole and down into the opposite side, pulling the thread tight every time. To secure it, repeat this three or four times. To avoid random holes, insert the needle in the same spot each time.
- **Thread button holes 3 and 4:** For the last two holes, thread up through one fabric and down into the other to form an "X" with the thread. After completing the "X," flip the fabric over and push the needle through

without passing through the button. This step involves inserting the needle between the fabric and the button back.

- **Wrap the button base with thread:** Flip the needle back over and wrap the thread around the button three or four times. Pull tight each time. This step generates room between the button and fabric to improve operation and ensures a tight stitch.

- **Tie the button back—reverse the needle:** Make a little backstitch by tugging the thread to form a loop. Knot this loop using your needle. Pull tight and repeat twice, then cut the thread.

Congrats! You've sewn a button!

## How to Clean a Bathroom

As much as you might not like it, you can and should help with cleaning around the house, including the bathroom. In the future (even if you have housekeepers), knowing your way around tools and products can't hurt. So, let's go clean your bathroom!

### CLEANING SUPPLIES

Here is a list of supplies to help you get ready for this boring (yet necessary) task:

- a container
- paper towels
- washcloths
- bins
- rag
- toilet paper

### CLEANING THE BATHROOM

Now that you know what you need, let's get to their uses. Here is a checklist you can follow when cleaning your bathroom (Mique, 2020):

- Make use of paper towels or clean washcloths to wipe down the counter.

- Apply soap to a towel and wipe off the sink.

- Wipe from top to bottom in an S-shaped motion. A newspaper is an excellent choice for cleaning mirrors.

- Depending on the surface, you may need to sweep or scrub. Bathrooms with tile floors should be mopped or cleansed by hand regularly.

- Use a soapy rag to scrub the shower, and then rinse it thoroughly. Maintaining a clean shower or tub can be time-consuming.

- Remove the trash and replace the liner.

You'll probably mess up the first couple of times. That's okay. Like learning anything new, it needs practice.

## Finding Your Way Around the Kitchen

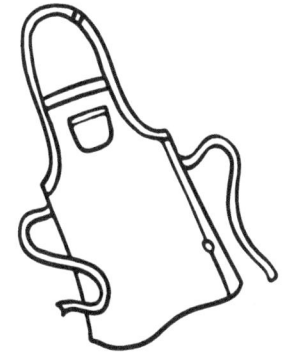

Do you like to cook? No, scrap that question. Do you love food?

I'm sure your answer would probably be yes, and your favorite food sprung to mind. If you don't know already, wouldn't it be awesome to be able to make your favorite meal whenever you want to? In this section, you'll learn how to handle yourself safely in the kitchen.

### SAFETY

Safety is essential in the kitchen. To avoid getting sick after eating, it's important to know how to shop for, prepare, and store food safely.

The following are a few points to remember regarding kitchen safety (Kids Health, n.d.-a):

### BUYING FOOD

Meat, dairy, eggs, and fish are perishable and should be among the last things you buy at the supermarket. Segregate raw meats from the rest of your groceries. Put these items in a cooler or insulated bag if your journey home will take more than an hour.

For safety, always examine the sell-by date on any packaged meat, poultry, or fish. Never purchase fish or meat that has an unusual odor or appearance, even if the quality is guaranteed to be "excellent."

Also, inspect the eggs you plan to buy. The best eggs are the ones that are spotless and have no cracks.

## REFRIGERATING/FREEZING

Cool your fridge to 5 °F (40 °C) and your freezer to 0 °F (-18 °C) or lower. No pathogens can flourish in such a chilly environment, making the food safe to eat.

Food storage tips:

- Most refrigerator doors don't keep eggs cold enough, so leave them in their cartons on a shelf.
- To avoid juices leaking on other items, store meat, poultry, and fish in plastic bags.
- If you won't eat for several days, freeze raw meat, poultry, or fish.

## PREPARING FRUITS AND VEGGIES

Have you ever bitten into a fruit only to taste worms? If not, then you probably wouldn't want to experience that. So, get rid of any fruit that looks like it has been spoiled.

To remove pesticides, filth, and bacteria, wash all produce under running water and dry it with a towel, even if you're going to peel it.

## COOKING RAW MEAT, POULTRY, FISH, AND EGGS

Don't clean raw chicken in the sink. Bacteria can be transferred when meat and poultry are washed. You should thaw meat, poultry, and fish in the refrigerator or microwave and then cook them right away.

Meat should be cooked completely so that its juices drain out.

## CLEANUP

To reduce bacteria, clean your kitchen and wash your hands often. Use paper towels and change them often to avoid spreading bacteria. Here are some more cleaning tips:

- Don't wait more than two hours to store your leftovers in the fridge after dinner. Throw away any food that has been in the fridge for more than three or four days.

- Soap and water can be used to clean the surfaces.
- Wash dishes, silverware, and cutting boards in the dishwasher or with hot, soapy water.
- Used, old cutting boards are a breeding ground for germs. Often disinfect surfaces like cutting boards, worktops, sinks, drains, and garbage disposals to prevent the spread of germs.
- Dish towels of thinner thickness tend to dry quicker. Towels and dish rags should be washed often.

## EXPIRY DATES

Food dates vary by region and serve different purposes.

- **Best Before:** This suggests the food's peak taste and quality date. It doesn't imply any purchase or safety date.
- **Use By:** This is the recommended eating date. It's fine to eat food that's a day or two over the use-by date, but you should assess its quality.
- **Sell By:** Not a safety date; this date helps retailers evaluate how long an item should stay on the shelf.

## HOW LONG ARE FOODS GOOD AFTER THE EXPIRATION DATE?

With the exception of infant formula, if the date (on your food) expires during home storage, a product should still be safe and wholesome if handled appropriately until the time spoiling is evident. Its smell, taste, or texture indicates spoilage.

Therefore, these are the recommended expiration dates for typical foods thrown out too early:

- **Canned food:** High-acid canned foods like tomatoes and citrus last 1.5 years. Low-acid canned goods—most everything else, including vegetables, meat, and fish—last up to 5 years. Though hygienic, canned foods lose flavor and texture with time. Avoid bulging, rusty, leaking, or deeply damaged cans, which are more likely to spoil. Store them at room temperature in a dark closet or pantry.
- **Frozen food:** Freezer items expire because flavor and texture degrade with time. Instead of touching frozen peas or corn, pour them out. Bacteria sur-

vive in the freezer but cannot multiply. After defrosting, microorganisms may be harmful if not cooked. Home-frozen meals should be discarded after 3–4 months. After that, they can freeze and absorb freezer tastes.

**Leftovers:** Most leftovers last up to 4 days. Seafood and mayonnaise-based dishes degrade faster, so eat them within two days. Don't leave food on the counter for more than 2 hours. Bacteria grow faster in room-temperature dishes.

## KITCHEN SAFETY

Safety is paramount to avoid sharp tools, electric devices, and extreme heat. These kitchen safety recommendations can help you learn about nutrition and cooking with safe instruments.

You'll feel more secure cooking with health and safety guidelines (Children's Wisconsin, n.d.).

## WATCH WHAT YOU'RE COOKING

Never walk away from a cooked meal. While you're cooking, stay close by. Avoid being sidetracked and keep your attention on the task at hand. Turn off the stove if you have to leave the room, even if it's just for a second.

Turn the pot handles inward and cook on the back burners of the stove.

## SHARP OBJECTS

Although it might seem silly at first, using a plastic knife with a peeled banana or watermelon can teach slicing, chopping, and dicing. Gradually introduce yourself to knives as you get better at chopping and slicing.

## STOVE SAFETY

Getting burned is never a good experience. It's safer to use the stove if you keep the handle of the pan away from the heat source.

## ESTABLISH A SAFETY ZONE

You should keep dish towels, paper or plastic bags, and draperies at least three feet away from the burner to prevent fires.

## MIND THE MICROWAVE

While taking things out of the oven or microwave, use hot pads at all times. Also, if you're boiling water, it's best to use a stovetop or an electric kettle.

Moreover, it is risky to switch on a microwave if there is nothing in it. The microwave magnetron can take in wavelengths even when it is empty. There is a risk that the microwave will either explode or start a fire.

## CHECK YOUR HOME FOR SAFETY

Your parents should put smoke alarms in every room of the house, including the kitchen, and test them frequently. Never turn off a smoke alarm. You should also learn how to use a fire extinguisher. Twice a year, go over your family's fire escape strategy and practice it.

Kitchen fires can spread rapidly. However, knowing how to handle them beforehand makes us feel better.

- If no adult is in the kitchen, call one.
- Smother tiny fires with baking soda.
- Remove oxygen from a stovetop pan fire by covering it.
- Leave the house and contact 911 if flames are huge and leaping.

## KITCHEN ACCIDENT TREATMENT

Before donning your apron and igniting your inner chef, study these kitchen safety and first aid precautions. It will make cooking safer.

## CUT TREATMENT

With sharp kitchen knives, you could cut your finger instead of the carrot if you're not careful.

Treating a kitchen knife cut:

- **Wash it:** Stop bleeding with a clean cloth or bandage. If you bleed, put another cloth on top.
- **Antibacterial ointment:** Dab this on minor cuts, then bandage and tape the area.

If the bleeding persists after five to twenty minutes, go to the hospital. If the cut is longer than half an inch, jagged, inflammatory, or leaks fluid, visit a doctor.

## BURN CARE

Turn pot handles toward the stove back to avoid burns.

First, identify the type: A first-degree burn only burns the outermost layer of skin. It hurts like a sunburn and has a red appearance. The charred area glows white when pressed.

- Remove clothing and jewelry near the burn to treat it. For 3–5 minutes, run cool water over the injury.
- Apply antibiotic ointment to your wound, not ice, oil, or butter. Bandage it cleanly. Healing can take 3–6 days.

A second-degree burn is very serious. It swells, blisters, gets red, and aches.

- Soak the burn for 15–30 minutes in cool water. Antibiotic cream prevents infection, and you can apply a sterile dressing.
- Change the dressing daily and check for infection (increased redness, swelling, discomfort, and pus).
- Don't scratch it when it itches.
- Healing takes 2–3 weeks.

A third-degree burn is a medical emergency.

- Call 911 or go to the closest ER after treating the wound with a cool, moist dressing.
- White or dark tissue covers this serious burn. It may not hurt, which means the skin nerves are injured.

Fall Treatment

Overflowing pots can cause slippery floors. If, however, you've fallen in the kitchen, do this:

- Before standing, check for injuries. Getting up in the wrong way could worsen the damage.
- Kneel slowly.
- Crawl to a chair and pull up.
- Call 911 or cry for help if you can't stand up.
- Avoid moving the swollen area if you suspect a fracture. Visit your doctor or the ER.

## EYE INJURY CARE

What if you get lemon juice in your eye? Get splattered with bleach (or another dangerous chemical) while cleaning? Here's what you do:

- Lean over the sink and splash lukewarm water over your eye. Flush for 15 minutes.
- Protect your other eye.
- Call your doctor if your eye remains inflamed after flushing.
- If your eye is cut, avoid washing or pressing.

## POISON

Swallowing even safe kitchen goods can be harmful. That's why all household cleansers and chemicals should be locked away unless in use. If, however, you're worried about ingesting something harmful, here's what you do immediately:

- Call 911 to report poisonings.
- To help doctors identify the chemical product eaten, bring it to the hospital.

It's not hard to stay safe in the kitchen. All you need is a clear head, sharp instincts, and the will to have a little fun cooking while being safe.

*Segue: In this chapter, we looked at the various skills that you can acquire for your home, like cleaning, ironing, cooking, and sewing. In the final chapter that follows, we'll talk about the wonders of driving and how to do so safely.*

# GET COOKING!

Part of being on your own involves preparing your own meals. As a beginner, you might not even know where to begin. A good place to start is by collecting some tried and true meal recipes, often handed down by friends or family. Use this space to fill them in and save them for future use. Or, better yet, start practicing now (with adult supervision).

# Chapter 8: The Responsibilities of Owning and Driving a Car

Imagine it: Getting your driver's license and your first car and taking a road trip to Malibu with your girls and sister. You're having a blast, and you've never felt so free in your life.

In truth, getting your license is one of the biggest milestones of independence that parents often worry about… understandably. They'll always be worrying about you on the road since they aren't driving you everywhere, but at the same time, they will be proud to see you growing up. Now, isn't that something that you want?

Well, in our final chapter, we'll talk about responsible driving and all you need to know about car maintenance as a girl. Freedom is great, but safety is better.

## Importance of Driving Responsibly

We've all watched a show or read a book where there was an awful car accident. Or maybe you've been in one or know someone close to you who has been. The sad reality is that these things happen, and you don't even have to be in the wrong to be in an accident. But the good thing is that you can do everything in your power to prevent one or lessen the impact if you weren't, indeed, in the wrong.

### TEEN DRIVERS STATISTICS

According to the National Center for Health Statistics, motor vehicle accidents are the main cause of death for those between the ages of 15 and 20. National studies of graded licensing indicated that robust legislation reduced fatal crash rates and insurance claim rates for young teen drivers. Raising the licensing age and restricting nighttime driving and teen passengers cut fatalities and insurance claims (Centers for Disease Control, 2022-b).

In 2020, motor vehicle crashes killed 2,800 US youths aged 13–19 and injured 227,000. Eight youths perished in motor vehicle crashes each day, and hundreds more were injured. In 2020, teen motor vehicle crash deaths cost approximately $40.7 billion in medical expenditures and life loss.

Here are some more alarming statistics (Centers for Disease Control, 2022-b):

- Motor vehicle crashes are highest among 16–19-year-olds.
- Male teens accounted for 2/3 of 2018 collision deaths. Since 1975, male teenage collision deaths have dropped 76% more than female ones at 59%.
- Drivers killed 63% of 16–19-year-old passenger car occupants in 2018.
- Teen collision deaths increased in July, May, June, September, and October 18.
- Friday, Saturday, and Sunday accounted for 52% of teen car crash deaths in 2018.
- Teenage motor vehicle crash deaths peaked between 9 p.m. to midnight in 2018.

This isn't meant to scare you or convince you not to drive. Remember when we said this was a milestone of independence? Well, it still is, and that includes driving safely, so you or anyone you know doesn't end up in these statistics.

## RISK FACTORS

So, what can put you at risk of an accident? Knowing these will help you prevent them from happening:

- inexperience
- nighttime and weekend driving
- rarely wearing seat belts
- distracted driving (interacting with passengers, cellphones, seeing something in the car, looking outside the vehicle, singing/dancing, grooming, reaching)
- speeding
- drinking alcohol before or while driving
- using drugs

## DRIVING SAFETY TIPS

Now that we know the serious part of driving, let's move on to easy and effective ways to ensure you're safe on the road. Consider these driving tips:

- Buckle up! Ensure everyone in the car is belted up as well.
- Follow speed limits. Speed reduces reaction time.
- Use your indicators! They alert other drivers.
- Always drive sober. Minors cannot drink.
- Focus on driving—the road and conditions.
- When driving, only drive. Reduce distractions.
- Keep music at a moderate level so you can hear things around you.
- Don't drive when you're upset.
- Drive without eating or drinking. These are distractions too.
- Find directions ahead of leaving.
- Leave early to lessen the "need for speed" (see what I did there?).

## Things You Should Know How to Do Before Getting Behind the Wheel

Having good car maintenance guarantees safety even more. So, it's vital to learn technical mechanics, even as a female.

Read the owner's and service handbook before performing any maintenance. Oil changes vary by make and age. You should have everything you need to maintain your vehicles. Make sure you understand and use these basic maintenance items:

- jumper cables
- spare tire
- air gauge
- penny (treadwear test) or tread gauge
- tire-fixing iron

- ratchet
- jack stand

## CHECK TIRE PRESSURE AND TREAD WEAR

You can easily maintain your car by monitoring tire pressure and tread wear. Before you drive, check tires for flats and underinflation. Tire pressure gauges are simple to use. These tips will help teens utilize a tire gauge:

- **Air pressure label:** Check the label on the frame inside the driver's side door for their car's suggested air pressure.
- **Tire pressure gauge:** Push the tire pressure gauge until a digital readout or a tiny marker rises to indicate tire pressure.
- **Verify the reading:** Replace the pressure gauge with the valve cap.
- **Air-up:** If tires are low, fill to the prescribed pressure.

The "penny testing" technique to test tread wear is a nifty gimmick. Keep a cent in your glove compartment so they can use it to measure the tire tread depth. If you can see Lincoln's head on a penny in the tread, your tread is too shallow, and the car is unsafe to drive.

Other equipment, such as digital tread depth gauges, can be used to measure tire wear.

## HOW TO CHANGE A TIRE

You can easily change tires with the correct tools and knowledge. However, you should only change tires when it's safe. Call a professional or roadside service if there is heavy traffic, extreme weather, or you lack the right tools. Before a traffic incident, practice at home.

You can follow these steps to change a tire:

- **Step 1:** Check the car's spare tire.
- **Step 2:** Research your location. Ensure your area is safe, and switch on your caution lights.
- **Step 3:** Use the parking brake and apply wheel wedges if you have them to prevent rolling.
- **Step 4:** Loosen the tire and remove the hubcap and tire lug bolts.

- **Step 5:** Carjack it. Check your car's handbook for jack positioning. Use a six-inch jack.

- **Step 6:** Remove lug nuts and tire. Unscrew and remove the flat tire.

- **Step 7:** Change the tire. Align the spare or new tire with the lug bolts and hand-tighten each bolt.

- **Step 8:** Fully lower your car and tighten all lug nuts.

- **Step 9:** Replace lids. Replace your wheel covers and stow your tools.

- **Step 10:** Verify the air pressure. Verify the air pressure on your spare or fresh tire. If air is required, drive slowly to a mechanic or gas station.

## HOW TO REPLACE WINDSHIELD WIPERS

To help see the road, keep windows and wipers clean. Replace windshield wipers when you notice streaks each time you wipe.

Follow this guide to help you replace your blades:

- **Verify blade size:** The owner's manual and most auto parts stores have this information. Each blade manufacturer has a book containing make, model, and year information.

- **Remove old blades:** Check your car's handbook for wiper blade removal instructions. Some "hook" the blades, while others snap them.

- **Replace blades:** Reverse the procedure you used to install the new blades after removing the old ones.

## CHECK FLUIDS

Maintaining automobile fluid levels is easy. You should make it a habit to check five fluids routinely. The following fluids are the most crucial to check and how often:

- **Engine oil:** You should check your engine oil monthly or every time you fill up at the gas station. Check engine oil:

    - Choose a dipstick. Find your engine oil dipstick in the owner's or service manual.

    - Remove and clean the dipstick.

- Replace the dipstick after placing it.
- Check engine oil fluid. No oil is needed if the fluid level is safe. However, fill it if it's low.

- **Coolant:** Check your coolant levels every six months before summer and winter. To check the amount of your coolant:
  - Find the coolant. It's usually in the radiator, but check your car's owner's or service manual.
  - After your automobile cools, check it.
  - Lift the radiator cap off.
  - Find the radiator's suggested coolant line. Fill if low.

- **Transmission fluid:** Check transmission fluid monthly. To check transmission fluid:
  - For accurate transmission fluid readings, run your car.
  - Check where the fluid is located by checking your owner's or service handbook.
  - Check quality, not quantity. Instead of level, check transmission fluid color and quality. Red fluid should not smell burned. Replace it if it's scorched or discolored. At the same time, avoid low transmission fluid.

- **Brakes fluid:** Brake fluid is another easy-to-check fluid. Every oil change should include a quality check. Brake fluid is usually housed in a driver-side engine compartment reservoir. Check the container for golden fluid. If it's brown or low, replace it or check the brakes.

- **Power-steering fluid:** Check power steering fluid monthly. Look for low power steering reservoir levels. If power steering fluid levels drop rapidly, take your car to a shop.

## JUMP-STARTING A CAR

Drivers should know how to jump-start a car safely. Both vehicles should be in neutral with vehicles off and emergency brakes engaged to start. First, clamp the red positive (+) line to the disabled vehicle's red battery terminal. Clamp the opposite end of that cable to the booster vehicle's red positive (+) connection. Next, clip the black negative (-) cable to the booster vehicle's black terminal.

Finally, connect the black negative cable's other end to a large, unpainted metal surface in the disabled vehicle's engine bay, away from the battery and engine. Start the disabled vehicle after connecting the cords. Run both vehicles for three minutes after starting.

## HOW TO RESPOND TO AN EMERGENCY

Every car needs emergency supplies. Jumper cables, tire pressure gauges, a flashlight, and danger signs are required. Just in case you get stranded, keep water and food like protein bars in the car. Blankets, jackets, candles, and matches can save your life on lengthy trips.

## HOW TO HANDLE THE "CHECK ENGINE" LIGHT

Check engine lights are warnings. Stop the car and call for help if the car feels odd, there are mechanical noises, tailpipe smoke, or electrical smells occur.

If there are no symptoms, take the car to a trustworthy shop for diagnosis.

## Car Dashboard Symbols

"I don't know what that light means!" you might find yourself saying before throwing a fit. But lights on the dashboard don't always indicate danger. Some of these issues are mechanical or linked to safety (like low tire pressure and engine temperature warnings). However, don't ever avoid them.

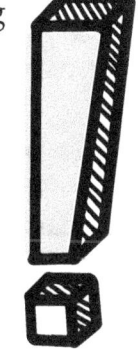

When the lights become green or blue, the system is ready to go. Your car's service indicator light will become orange or yellow if it needs attention. There is less of a sense of urgency here than there would be with, say, flashing red lights.

When you see red, you should take immediate action. Red dashboard lights indicate danger and serve as reminders to fasten safety belts or alert mechanical problems (such as an overheating engine). Stop and check it out. If you can't check it on your own, call someone to help. You risk damaging or wrecking your car if you keep going.

The best source of information about your vehicle is the manual written just for it.

## WHAT TO DO AFTER AN ACCIDENT

Many new drivers have little accidents; thankfully, no one is usually hurt. However, accident response is crucial. Turn on your flashers and safely exit traffic if the vehicle is drivable. Then, immediately report it to the police. Exchange insurance data with the other driver without discussing the accident or fault. Take pictures and take notes.

## DRIVING IN RAIN AND SNOW

In rain and snow, reduce your speed to leave greater space between you and the car ahead. Learn how to manage skids. Practice skidding reactions on a snow-covered vacant parking lot. Learn how to drive with reduced traction and vision if a car hydroplanes on a rain puddle.

Hopefully, you'll never encounter an accident or roadside emergency, but being ready will keep them safe.

## THE IMPORTANCE OF PREVENTIVE MAINTENANCE

Preventative maintenance keeps a car operating and keeps you safe. Regular oil changes, tire rotation, alignment, and tune-ups are necessary. For early auto care habits, schedule preventative maintenance and tune-ups in advance.

# What to Do When You Get Pulled Over by a Cop

Cops can be intimidating, especially if they see that you're a young driver. Getting pulled over for the first time can give you the chills, but knowing how to handle the situation will ensure that you'll be fine. So, in this final section, we'll take a quick look at what to do when a cop stops you without escalating the situation.

## PULLOVER PROCEDURE

Driving is a regular police encounter for teens. If the cops pull you over, do these 10 things:

- Show the police your license, registration, and insurance. The police can verify your identity and car's compliance with the state's driving laws by inspecting these documents.

- Don't let cops search the car. Your car is private. Know that the police need a judge-signed search warrant in order to search your car, with few exceptions. You should refuse to let the cops check the car, even though it's hard. Drivers who consent to police searches do not need warrants.

- Do not discuss mobile phone use, alcohol, marijuana, and so on. These are illegal for teens. You should avoid these criminal behaviors. You have the same right to silence, regardless of guilt, so use it! Tell the police officer you won't answer such questions without a lawyer, and tell them that you're calling your parents immediately.

- You must exit the car if the cops ask. The police officer may ask drivers to exit their cars for interrogation, depending on the stop. You must obey. If you don't, the police will arrest you and may use force to make you cooperate.

- Refuse physical coordination exams. Police might require drivers to undergo multiple physical coordination tests if they suspect alcohol or drug use. The police officer's assessment of the driver's performance is subjective, yet prosecutors often cite it as proof of guilt. Teens should decline these tests.

- Refuse a breathalyzer. The police might request a breath test from you to gather evidence against you. You shouldn't take breath tests.

- If feasible, record the interaction on your phone. You can videotape police interactions (or have your friends do so). It will preserve what happened. The police officer's "official" version may prevail.

- Show your hands and never run. This is critical. Even if you'll get in trouble, don't drive away or escape from the police. Running from the police makes things worse. They will use force. You should also show the police officer your hands while in the car. Police may suspect a weapon if they cannot see a person's hands. You will want to reassure cops. Empty hands work best.

- Say nothing more. Don't talk to the police about your behavior. Teens sometimes assume they can solve problems with words. It's different with the police. The cops will use your statements against you. You can remain silent. Use this powerful right.

- Request a lawyer immediately. The police may mistreat you. Ask your parents about getting a lawyer.

This might all seem a bit stiff, but don't let this discourage you from driving. As long as you do what's right and lawful, follow the driving tips, and ensure your car is in the best fitness, you'll be driving without issues for a lifetime.

*Segue: In this last chapter, we discussed all you need to know about having and maintaining a car, safety tips, and what to do in difficult driving situations.*

# WHERE YA HEADED?

Your first experiences behind the wheel are exhiliarating and you'll want to test your newfound freedom. Think about some places you intend to visit when the time comes (and with your parents permission). Where will you go? Who will you take? What kind of precautions will you need to take?

# Conclusion

Growing up can be hard, and it doesn't usually come with a manual for knowing what to do at every single change in your life. But one thing's for sure: It will happen, and there's nothing we can do to stop it. So, it really is important that we make the most of the knowledge gained in every aspect of life and learn essential life skills that will benefit us in the long run.

Knowing your worth, loving yourself, surrounding yourself with the right people, and being confident in everything you do and choose is perhaps the most important thing you can ever learn as a teen. Self-love is above all, and once you love yourself and fill your life with positivity and strength, you'll be just fine in this race called life. It's also important that you take care of yourself, knowing your body and everything you need, which will, in turn, help you to be mannerable and kind to others around you, even strangers.

Liking someone is another thing teenage life throws at you, and you might find yourself trying so hard to let go but simply can't. The trick is just to go with it in the right way, never degrading or limiting yourself and who you are, but at the same time exploring your feelings safely.

You'll also need to learn how to be a proud young woman as you grow up, and this includes getting a job, knowing your way around your house and basic chores, and of course, taking your first car for a spin around the block.

So, growing up won't necessarily be a walk in the park, but it shouldn't be a burden. Having essential life skills and knowing what to do in certain situations is how you tackle this life, no matter who you are. You'll be a wonderful adult one day, but remember to enjoy the day of your youth and embrace every lesson that comes your way.

# Glossary

**Detrimental:** Something or someone that is undesirable or harmful.

**Malware:** A type of software that is designed to interfere with the functioning of your computer.

**Mediocre:** Something of low quality or value.

**Nifty:** Attractive or pleasing.

**Paramount:** Being superior to others.

**Perception:** Having awareness of environmental elements through physical sensation.

**Predetermined:** To impose a direction or tendency beforehand.

**Unpasteurized:** Not pasteurized (partial sterilization of a substance at a temperature that destroys organisms without chemically altering the substance).

# References

Adcock, D. (2021, April 16). 10 signs you're in a toxic friendship. The Source. https://www.thesource.org/post/10-signs-youre-in-a-toxic-friendship

Adhav, L. (2020, July 31). Here's how to sew on a button if you've always wanted to learn. Cosmopolitan. https://www.cosmopolitan.com/style-beauty/fashion/a33481891/how-to-sew-button/

A guide for menstrual products for teens. (n.d.). Green Valley. https://gvobgyn.com/menstrual-products-for-teens/

Anzilotti, A. W. (n.d.). Tampons, pads and other period supplies. Teens Health. https://kidshealth.org/en/teens/supplies.html

Arzt, N. (2021, August 26). Toxic friends: 13 signs of a toxic friendship. Choosing Therapy. https://www.choosingtherapy.com/toxic-friends/

Asenov, E. (2022, September 8). Resume for a 16-year-old. Enhancv. https://enhancv.com/blog/resume-for-a-16-year-old/

Avoid teenage money problems with these top financial tips for teens. (2020, March 23). Firefighter Center. https://www.ffcommunity.com/financial-tips-for-teens

Barclay, L. (n.d.). Recipes for teenagers. Good Food. https://www.bbcgoodfood.com/howto/guide/recipes-teenagers

Battles, M. (2021, January 12). 15 ways to practice positive self-talk for success. Lifehack. https://www.lifehack.org/504756/self-talk-determines-your-success-15-tips

Begum, J. (2021, November 24). How to trim your nails. WebMD. https://www.webmd.com/beauty/how-to-trim-your-nails

Belludi, N. (2007, November 3). Etiquette: Protocol of introducing people. Right Attitudes. https://www.rightattitudes.com/2007/11/03/etiquette-protocol-introducing-people/

Birt, J. (2020, April 3). How to do introductions (with examples and tips). Indeed. https://www.indeed.com/career-advice/interviewing/how-to-do-introductions

BrainyQuote. (n.d.). E. E. Cummings quotes. https://www.brainyquote.com/quotes/e_e_cummings_161593

Brock, C. (2021, November 7). Teens: Want to start wearing makeup? Read this first. Budget Fashionista. https://www.thebudgetfashionista.com/archive/teen-makeup-tips/

Budgeting for teens. (n.d.). Copper. https://www.getcopper.com/guide/budgeting

Butler, T. (2018, November 20). Teen dating advice. Love to Know. https://dating.lovetoknow.com/Teen_Dating

Campano, L. (2022, August 5). 10 signs you're in a toxic friendship. Seventeen. https://www.seventeen.com/life/friends-family/a40785362/toxic-friendships-signs/

Centeno, A. (2022, August 1). 5 tricky tip situations, tipping rules, how to leave gratuity correctly, takeout & bad service. Real Men Real Style. https://www.realmenrealstyle.com/how-to-tip/

Centers for Disease Control and Prevention. (2022-a, February 28). Fast facts: Preventing teen dating violence. https://www.cdc.gov/violenceprevention/intimatepartnerviolence/teendatingviolence/fastfact.html

Centers for Disease Control and Prevention. (2022-b, November 21). Teen drivers and passengers: Get the facts. https://www.cdc.gov/transportationsafety/teen_drivers/teendrivers_factsheet.html

Center for Women's Health. (2019, July 17). What do I do if I accidentally cut myself while shaving? https://youngwomenshealth.org/askus/cut-myself-while-shaving/

Children's Wisconsin. (n.d.). Teens in the kitchen. https://childrenswi.org/-/media/chwlibrary/files/childrens-and-the-community/families-and-clients/safety-center/cw_teens-in-the-kitchen.pdf

Chloe. (n.d.). 7 Valid and surprising reasons you shouldn't wear makeup. All Womens Talk. https://makeup.allwomenstalk.com/valid-and-surprising-reasons-you-shouldnt-wear-makeup/

Cook, V. & Blacklock, A. (n.d.). 10 essential financial lessons for teens. Medi-Share. https://www.medishare.com/blog/10-essential-money-lessons-every-teen-should-learn#Number-9

Daniel, P. (n.d.). Important restaurant etiquette and table manners we all should get our teen started with. Parent Circle. https://www.parentcircle.com/eating-out-etiquette-for-teens/article

De Jong, J., & Pradhan, S. (2022, March 21). Getting your period: What is a 'normal' menstrual cycle for teens and preteens? UChicago Medicine. https://www.uchicagomedicine.org/forefront/pediatrics-articles/getting-your-period-normal-menstrual-cycle-teens-preteens

Doleac, S. (n.d.). Kitchen safety for kids: 15 smart tips for safe cooking. Primal Peak. https://primalpeak.com/kitchen-safety-for-kids/

Doumbia, A. (2022, September 16). How to take care of your teen's curly hair. Wuli Grooming. https://www.wuligrooming.com/blogs/journal/how-to-take-care-of-your-teens-curly-hair

Doyle, A. (2022, March 31). Teen resume examples with writing tips. The Balance. https://www.thebalancemoney.com/part-time-job-resume-example-for-a-teen-2063248

Doyle, A. (2022, December 26). Teen jobs interview questions, answers, and tips. The Balance. https://www.thebalancemoney.com/teen-job-interview-questions-and-best-answers-2063882#toc-what-to-bring-with-you

Duszyński, M. (2023, January 10). How to introduce yourself professionally and casually—examples. Zety. https://zety.com/blog/how-to-introduce-yourself

EHE Health. (2020, December). Top 5 important reasons you should use sunscreen. https://ehe.health/blog/always-wear-sunscreen/

Ehmke, R. (2023, February 2). Teens and romantic relationships. Child Mind Institute. https://childmind.org/article/how-to-help-kids-have-good-romantic-relationships/

Eriks Dental Group. (n.d.). Natural hacks for combating bad breath. https://eriksdentalgroup.com/natural-hacks-for-combating-bad-breath/

Eva, A. L. (2018, May 21). Five ways to help teens feel good about themselves. Greater Good Magazine. https://greatergood.berkeley.edu/article/item/five_ways_to_help_teens_feel_good_about_themselves

Evar, E. (2018, March 23). How to deal with nicks and cuts from shaving. Beau

Brummell. https://beaubrummellformen.com/blogs/blog/how-to-deal-with-nicks-and-cuts-from-shaving

Ferreira, M. (2017, February 27). 11 hacks to beat B.O. Healthline. https://www.healthline.com/health/beat-b-o-and-smell-fresh-hacks

Forte, C., & Kim, J. (2021, May 7). How to iron a shirt. Good Housekeeping. https://www.goodhousekeeping.com/clothing/a35301390/how-to-iron-a-shirt/

Goodreads. (n.d.). Quotable quote. https://www.goodreads.com/quotes/203299-when-you-become-a-teenager-you-step-onto-a-bridge

Good News Network. (2018, July 24). "You are very powerful, provided you know how powerful you are." –Yogi Bhajan. https://www.goodnewsnetwork.org/yogi-bhajan-quote-on-knowing-your-power/

Gordon, S. (2022, November 21). 17 dating tips for teens and parents. Very Well Family. https://www.verywellfamily.com/safe-dating-tips-for-teens-and-parents-5100832

Gross, E. L. (2022, May 18). 10 signs your friendship is toxic and how to deal with it. Well and Good. https://www.wellandgood.com/signs-of-toxic-friendship/

Hair care tips for teens. (n.d.). Web MD. https://teens.webmd.com/hair-care-tips

Hand sewing: Thread the needle & tie the knot. (2009, May 28). Sew4Home. https://sew4home.com/hand-sewing-thread-the-needle-tie-the-knot/

Handy shaving guide for girls. (n.d.). Joy + Glee. https://joyandglee.com/blog/shaving-tips-teen-girls

Health for Teens. (2022, June 24). 5 simple tips to make friends. https://www.healthforteens.co.uk/relationships/friendships/5-simple-tips-to-make-friends/

Herrity, J. (2020, January 3). Self-introduction tips with samples and examples. Indeed. https://www.indeed.com/career-advice/career-development/self-introduction-tips

Higuera, V. P (2022, December 28). How to set up a savings account for a teenager. My Bank Tracker. https://www.mybanktracker.com/savings/faq/

how-to-set-up-a-savings-account-for-a-teenager-297534#:~:text=Minor%27s%20can%20only%20open%20a,long%20as%20it%20is%20open

How to handle peer pressure. (n.d.). FairFax County Public Schools. https://www.fcps.edu/student-wellness-tips/peer-pressure

Indeed Editorial Team. (2020-a, February 25). 9 tips to improve your professional handshake. Indeed. https://www.indeed.com/career-advice/career-development/professional-handshake

Indeed Editorial Team. (2020-b, February 25). Resume examples for teens: Templates and writing tips. Indeed. https://www.indeed.com/career-advice/resumes-cover-letters/resume-examples-for-teens

Indeed Editorial Team. (2021, November 3). How to find a job as a teenager (plus benefits and job types). Indeed. https://www.indeed.com/career-advice/finding-a-job/how-to-find-job-as-teenager

Kamboj, S. (n.d.). How to shop for a teenager's bra. Riti Riwaz. https://www.ritiriwaz.com/how-to-shop-for-a-teenagers-bra/

Kids Health. (n.d.-a). Food safety. https://kidshealth.org/en/parents/food-safety.html

Kids Health. (n.d.-b). How to handle peer pressure. https://kidshealth.org/en/kids/peer-pressure.html

Kim, Y., & Campano, L. (2022, November 11). How to tell your crush you like them without making things weird. Seventeen. https://www.seventeen.com/love/dating-advice/a26324989/how-to-tell-someone-you-like-them/

Kline, S. (2016, May 11). Confidence hack for teens: Self-talk (3 tips to help guide your teen). Linkedin. https://www.linkedin.com/pulse/1-confidence-hack-teens-self-talk-3-tips-help-guide-your-sheryl-kline/

Lake, R. (2022, July 5). Budgeting for teens: What you need to know. The Balance. https://www.thebalancemoney.com/how-to-teach-your-teen-about-budgeting-4160105

Leverette, M. (2022-a, May 7). How to do laundry in 10 easy steps. The Spruce. https://www.thespruce.com/how-to-do-laundry-2146149

Leverette, M. (2022-b, January 12). How to unshrink a shrunken sweater. The Spruce. https://www.thespruce.com/saving-a-shrunken-wool-sweat-

Leverette, M. (2022-c, August 14). How to remove stains from clothes. The Spruce. https://www.thespruce.com/how-to-remove-dye-bleeding-stains-2146663

Leverette, M. (2022-d, May 21). How to clean clothes and carpet to remove marks. The Spruce. https://www.thespruce.com/how-to-remove-ironing-scorch-marks-2146664

Maaree. (2018, October 4). 9 clear signs that your bra doesn't fit you. https://www.maaree.com/blogs/news/9-clear-signs-that-your-bra-doesnt-fit-you

Malek, F. A. (2021, January 5). 12 makeup tips every teenager would want to know and products to try. Fustany. https://fustany.com/en/beauty/makeup/simple-makeup-tips-for-teenage-beginners

McCConnell, L. (2022, September 1). 69 first date ideas you'll actually find fun. Teen Vogue. https://www.teenvogue.com/story/first-date-ideas

Mique. (2020, November 2). How to clean bathroom. 30 Days. https://www.thirtyhandmadedays.com/spring-cleaning-how-to-clean-the-bathroom-with-printable-checklists/

Mitchell, J. (2021, September 7). How having good manners benefits your entire life. Homeschool Adventure. https://homeschooladventure.com/blog/benefits-and-importance-of-good-manners-in-life/

Noah. (2022, August 20). How long can you keep canned tomatoes. Power Up Cook. https://powerupcook.com/how-long-can-you-keep-canned-tomatoes/

Pai, R. (2022, December 11). 21 cute ways to ask a guy out. Mom Junction. https://www.momjunction.com/articles/how-to-ask-a-guy-out_00719463/

Patwal, S. (2022, December 30). 26 easy and healthy recipes for teenagers to cook. Mom Junction. https://www.momjunction.com/articles/easy-recipes-cooking-for-teenagers_00782578/

Paulus, N. (2022, December 12). How to build a personal financial foundation for teens. Money Geek. https://www.moneygeek.com/financial-planning/personal-finance-for-teens/

Period hacks: How to feel better on your period. (n.d). Tampax. https://tampax.com/en-us/period-health/how-to-feel-better-on-your-period/

Real Simple Editors. (2023, January 30). It's usually safe to eat food past the expiration date—here's how to know when it's ok. Real Simple. https://www.realsimple.com/food-recipes/shopping-storing/food/food-expiration-dates-guidelines-chart

Robert Kiyosaki quotes. (n.d.). AZ Quotes. https://www.azquotes.com/quote/527418

Salek, E. (2019, January 25). 8 strategies to handle peer pressure. Center For Parent and Teen Communication. https://parentandteen.com/say-no-peer-pressure/

Seventeen.com Editors. (2023, January 5). 39 first date ideas that won't break the bank. Seventeen. https://www.seventeen.com/love/dating-advice/advice/g1079/cheap-date-ideas-for-teens/

Signs you're wearing the wrong bra. (n.d.). Web MD. https://www.webmd.com/women/ss/slideshow-signs-wearing-the-wrong-bra

Sinha, R. (2022, December 26). 25 essential and simple beauty tips for teenage girls to look flawless. Simple Craze. https://www.stylecraze.com/articles/12-beauty-tips-that-every-teen-should-know/

Skin Cancer Foundation. (2022, July). All about sunscreen. https://www.skincancer.org/skin-cancer-prevention/sun-protection/sunscreen/

Sullivan, K. (2015, March 2). Yes ladies, you can just shave your mustache. Allure. https://www.allure.com/story/shave-moustache

Sulpy, E. (2022, December 8). How to teach basic car maintenance to your teen. Jerry. https://getjerry.com/advice/how-to-teach-basic-car-maintenance-to-your-teen-by-elaine-sulpy#basic-car-maintenance

Taylor, S., & Diffey, B. (2022). Simple dosage guide for suncreams will help users. BMJ. 324(7352). https://doi.org/10.1136/bmj.324.7352.1526/a

Teen driving statistics. (n.d). Rocky Mountain Insurance Information Association. http://www.rmiia.org/auto/teens/Teen_Driving_Statistics.asp

Teens Health. (n.d.). All about periods. https://kidshealth.org/en/teens/menstruation.html

Teens Health. (n.d). How to break up respectfully. https://kidshealth.org/en/teens/break-up.html

10 things every teen should know about auto care. (2016, August 9). InMotion Auto Care. https://www.inmotionautocare.com/blog/10-things-every-teen-should-know-about-auto-care

The Strive. (n.d). 14 best confidence hacks to help you feel confident fast. https://thestrive.co/life-hacks-for-building-confidence-fast/

Thomas, A. J. (n.d). How to make friends as a teenager. Love to Know. https://teens.lovetoknow.com/how-make-friends

Top 5 hacks for fresher breath. (2018, July 18). Bamboo Dental. https://www.bamboodental.co.uk/news/top-5-hacks-fresher-breath/

Top hair care tips for teenagers and young adults. (2021, June 17). Teenology. https://teenology.com/blogs/news/hair-care-tips-for-teens-young-adults

Tucker, J. (2022, May 28). 10 tips for tween & teen girls who are ready to shave. Moms. https://www.moms.com/shaving-tips-tween-teen-girls/#never-share-the-razor

Uplifted Lingerie. (2021, June 21). How to choose a bra for a teenager—everything to consider. https://www.upliftedlingerie.co.uk/how-to-choose-bra-for-a-teenager/

Vandal, J. (2023, February 2). The ultimate guide to tipping etiquette in every situation—and when not to tip. Real Simple. https://www.realsimple.com/work-life/money/money-etiquette/tipping-etiquette-guide

VanSomeren, L. (2022, March 12). Rule of thumb: How big should your emergency fund be? The Balance. https://www.thebalancemoney.com/is-your-emergency-fund-too-big-4142617

Watson, S. (2020, October 19). First aid for kitchen accidents. WebMD. https://www.webmd.com/first-aid/kitchen-first-aid

WebMD. (2020, September 10). Body odor. https://www.webmd.com/skin-problems-and-treatments/preventing-body-odor

WebMD. (2022, December 7). Shaving tips for teen girls. https://teens.webmd.com/shaving-tips-girls

Wexler, L. (2017, January 3). Manners the traffic lights that guide human interaction. LinkedIn. https://www.linkedin.com/pulse/manners-traffic-lights-guide-human-interaction-lynn-wexler?trk=mp-reader-card

What should your child do if they get pulled over by the police? (n.d). Ruane Attorneys at Law. https://www.ruaneattorneys.com/connecticut-criminal/juvenile-defense/teenagers-and-interacting-with-the-police/what-should-your-child-do-if-they-get-pulled-over-by-the-police/

Whetat, N. (2020, September 3). Practical relationship advice for teenage girls. Issues of Love. https://issuesoflove.com/practical-relationship-advice-for-teenage-girls/

Wilson, A. (2022, August 18). Iron clothes like a pro with these hacks. Better Homes and Gardens. https://www.bhg.com/homekeeping/laundry-linens/clothes/how-to-iron/

Witmer, D. (2020, May 13). Teaching your teen to use their manners. Very Well Family. https://www.verywellfamily.com/manners-your-teen-should-use-and-how-to-teach-them-2608864

Yarborough, K. (2023, January 13). How often should you be cleaning your makeup brushes? Southern Living. https://www.southernliving.com/fashion-beauty/beauty-makeup/how-often-to-clean-makeup-brushes#:~:text=So%2C%20how%20often%20should%20you,every%20two%20weeks%20is%20preferable

Youth Central (n.d.). How to write a cover letter. https://www.youthcentral.vic.gov.au/jobs-and-careers/applying-for-a-job/what-is-a-cover-letter/how-to-write-a-cover-letter

Zechman, M. (n.d.). 20 important table manners for teens and tweens. Education Possible. https://educationpossible.com/table-manners-for-teens/

Image References

Adriane, M. (2017, May 17). Sunset strip sidewalk sign. [Image]. Unsplash. https://unsplash.com/photos/muS2RraYRuQ

Antoniadou, N. (2020, April 16). Stay safe, Covid-19, quarantine. [Image]. Unsplash. https://unsplash.com/photos/07rYS9_iEkc

Content Pixie. (2020, June 14). Facial cleansing tools and massage jade blender. [Image]. Unsplash. https://unsplash.com/photos/0z4h9qneDMA

Dumlao, N. (2017, December 14). [Couple sitting on a field facing a city]. [Image]. Unsplash. https://unsplash.com/photos/EdULZpOKsUE

Freestocks. (2018, February 5). [Pink hearts lights decor]. [Image]. Unsplash https://unsplash.com/photos/r_oV6smBBYk

Goodnotes. (2022, May 13). Budgeting on an iPad with GoodNotes at a window. [Image]. Unsplash. https://unsplash.com/photos/y356dQxeMn0

Grey, A. (2019, April 30). An example of gender non-conformity. Bink, drag kid persona. [Image]. Unsplash. https://unsplash.com/photos/wx3JOq0Xbh4

Kalonji, P. (2022, January 26). Makeup. [Image]. Unsplash. https://unsplash.com/photos/LH74lRYvBY4

Katzenberger, P. (2019, August 11). Mercedes Benz CLA 200. [Image]. Unsplash. https://unsplash.com/photos/sXOlZ7okg0c

Kehmeier, A. (2020, January 7). [View of two persons hands]. [Image]. Unsplash. https://unsplash.com/photos/lyiKExA4zQA

Lark, B. (2017, January 21). It's my favorite mug. It just is. [Image]. Unsplash. https://unsplash.com/photos/nMffL1zjbw4

Lark, B. (2017, September 20). A warm cozy kitchen is the perfect antidote for autumn. [Image]. Unsplash. https://unsplash.com/photos/wMzx2nBdeng

Nasir, M. S. (2021, February 17). Sewing day. [Image]. Unsplash. https://unsplash.com/photos/sFubXOglx7g

Neel, A. (2017, July 11). [MacBook Pro, white ceramic mug and black smartphone on table]. [Image]. Unsplash. https://unsplash.com/photos/cckf4TsHAuw

Rosly, R. (2019, December 29). Calligraphy quotes with black background. [Image]. Unsplash. https://unsplash.com/photos/B-vYrlcXzkA

Spiske, M. (2018, November 10). Boss and employee or exclusion of a person because of their appearance or ethnicity? [Image]. Unsplash. https://unsplash.com/photos/QozzJpFZ2lg

Sprat, A. (2020, February 26). Laundry basket full of clean clothes. [Image]. Unsplash. https://unsplash.com/photos/5TfCI4nj6B4

Taissin, A. (2020, December 13). Piggy bank. [Image]. Unsplash. https://unsplash.com/photos/Dc2SRspMak4

The Female Company. (2020, February 4). Designbox with hands, tampon-box, packaging. [Image]. Unsplash. https://unsplash.com/photos/Z3W-FX9qzX8U

Wisz, B. (2019, May 1). [Person holding credit card swipe machine]. [Image]. Unsplash. https://unsplash.com/photos/-JJg90OAnWI

www.ingramcontent.com/pod-product-compliance
Lightning Source LLC
Chambersburg PA
CBHW081357130526
44581CB00013B/111